Defiant Daughters

Defiant Daughters

21 WOMEN ON ART, ACTIVISM, ANIMALS, AND *THE SEXUAL POLITICS OF MEAT*

Edited by KARA DAVIS *and* WENDY LEE

With an Introduction by CAROL J. ADAMS

Lantern Books

A DIVISION OF BOOKLIGHT, INC. | NEW YORK

2013

Lantern Books

128 Second Place

Brooklyn, NY 11231

lanternbooks.com

Printed in the United States of America

The cover illustration is a papercutting by Jenny Lee Fowler (jennyleefowler.com).
Designed by J. Lops
Proceeds from the sale of this book go to Our Hen House (ourhenhouse.org).

LIBRARY OF CONGRESS CATALOGING-IN-PUBLICATION DATA

Defiant daughters : 21 women on art, activism, animals,
and The sexual politics of meat / edited by Kara Davis and Wendy Lee ;
with an introduction by Carol J. Adams.

pages cm

ISBN 978-1-59056-419-6 (pbk. : alk. paper) — ISBN 978-1-59056-420-2 (ebook)

1. Adams, Carol J. Sexual politics of meat.
2. Animal welfare. 3. Feminism. 4. Feminist theory.
I. Davis, Kara, 1970– II. Lee, Wendy, 1976–
HV4708.A25D44 2013
179'.3—dc23

2012045759

FSC

www.fsc.org

MIX

Paper from
responsible sources

FSC® C011935

Contents

Foreword

Recently, I had dinner with several young feminists in Portland. They were part of Feminist Agenda PDX, which was hosting the slideshow I developed to illustrate the concepts in my book *The Sexual Politics of Meat: A Feminist-Vegetarian Critical Theory.*

Over a delicious vegan meal, they asked questions about what it was like to be a feminist in the 1970s and 1980s. I laughed and said to them, "If only I could go back in time to 1980 and talk to the twenty-nine-year-old Carol Adams who was struggling with so much and feeling like such a failure for not having figured out how to write her book. If only I could go back and tell her, 'Don't worry, Carol, you are going to be eating delicious vegan food in Portland with young feminists in 2012.'"

Or, if only I could tell her, "You are going to meet bloggers, and activists, and thinkers, and founders of new museums, and writers, and filmmakers. You are going to learn their stories because they will contribute to an anthology that you can't even begin to imagine existing, because you haven't been able to imagine your own book existing."

I met someone else in Portland, who had been involved for

years in getting legislation passed to protect animals. She told me that when *The Sexual Politics of Meat* came out, she and her Wellesley classmates exclaimed, "Yes, someone gets it!" She said it was as though I had written it just for them.

In fact, I did. I wrote the book I needed when I became a vegetarian in 1974. In writing what I had needed to read, I ended up writing what others needed too.

But back then, I wasn't aware of that. An unpublished writer does not know what it is like to have readers. It is even hard for her to imagine some future state in which she will have readers.

While writing *The Sexual Politics of Meat*, three concerns possessed me.

First, I needed to respond to an intuition that I had had in 1974 that oppressions were interconnected. Over the next fifteen years, I tried to make sense of all the information I was gathering about the interconnections of sex, race, class, and species. I was acutely aware of my alienation from the dominant culture. Identifying why I was alienated meant answering the question, "What is my alternate vision?" This required years of thinking and reading and getting miles of activism under my belt.

Second, I wanted to convey to feminists the immense world of injustice we end up participating in if we think feminism only addresses oppression among human beings.

Third, I needed to show the animal rights movement, and the vegetarian and vegan worlds, that all of our efforts to bring about change for animals would fail if we didn't have a feminist viewpoint.

I had to figure out what I was trying to say and then how to say it—two entirely different things. When, thirteen years into this project, I discovered the literary concept of the absent referent and realized how it could be politicized to describe the disappearance of a subject through objectification and violence, my very own feminist-vegan theory erupted.

An author—well, this author—takes her life and experiences and thoughts and alienations and vision, and over fifteen years she worries them together in her mind and her body, in her activism and in her dreaming, and finally completes her book. Out of her fleshly existence, out of the deeply-felt and then lived insights, she crafts words. Flesh becomes words.

I received my first published copy of *The Sexual Politics of Meat* in late December 1989. Something I had been thinking about for fifteen years was now realized in a hardcover book.

Before publication, the manuscript went through scores of drafts, including at least three major overhauls. When it was finally published I thought, "Well, that is done. Take a rest and then figure out what you want to do next."

But my readers had a different understanding.

A book goes out into the world, and if the author is lucky, it does the work she envisioned for it: altering consciousness and enabling change. If the author is really lucky, the book actually does more than the author ever dreamt of.

I am one lucky author. I have gone from not knowing what it was like to have readers to being given the gift of connection and a relationship with readers. I am a different person, not only because I stuck with a vision for a book for fifteen years, but because as others read *The Sexual Politics of Meat*, they responded with their stories and their insights and their activism. Every day I hear from a reader by mail, email, Facebook, or Twitter who wants me to know what *The Sexual Politics of Meat* has meant to her or him.

At some point in the early 1990s, my editor, Evander Lomke, observed that *The Sexual Politics of Meat* had become a "classic." His definition of "classic" was "a book you are expected to know about, but no longer are expected to read."

Again, I am one lucky author. *The Sexual Politics of Meat* has never gone out of print and continues to find new readers.

If a writer turns flesh into words, readers who "get it," who enter into the vision, who have been looking for how to make sense of the connections they are seeing—or suddenly understand that there are connections among things they care about—transform words into flesh.

A book changes our way of looking at the world, and everything else follows. By identifying some of the ways that the violence of the dominant culture impacts us and asserting that we aren't powerless against it, *The Sexual Politics of Meat* helps readers think themselves toward new possibilities, new ways of living.

The dominant culture often defines the success of a book by its appearance on a bestseller list. That measures sales, not readers. My book is more likely to be handed from friend to friend, or family member to family member. I know it was shared in a Pennsylvania jail after a protest against a pigeon shoot. It is a book that affirms others in their resistance.

Restoring the absent referent—refusing the metaphors of oppression; boycotting the disappearance of the living animal through dead flesh, dairy, and eggs—also includes recognizing our own wonderful selves: who we are, what we believe, and how we, uniquely, want to touch and repair the world. While this insight offers an opportunity for healing, I never anticipated that my book would be a vehicle of healing for its readers. One of the greatest gifts I have received as a result of being the author of *The Sexual Politics of Meat* is being trusted with deeply personal stories in which someone who experienced fragmentation now experiences healing.

The pages that follow contain twenty-one wonderfully complex, beautifully written, evocative, painful, intimate stories. As the writers tell us their own stories—turning flesh into words—they trust us, their readers, to hear and to understand. I celebrate these women writers, feminist-vegans and becoming-vegans. I rejoice in survival, and I love the creativity that has been brought to their lives, as well as their sense of purpose and vision and feminist fierceness. They describe how reading *The Sexual Politics of Meat* is entangled in a larger story, one that is uniquely their own.

In some ways, I am not unlike the women whose stories are contained in this book because *The Sexual Politics of Meat* changed my life, too.

Within a week of its appearance, I began to hear from readers. They sent me examples of the sexual politics of meat that they saw in the world around them, confirming my analysis. My readers were so happy to have someone to whom they could send these oppressive images and stories, someone who would see and hear and interpret. I felt challenged to respond. They would say, "I see this…" or "This happened to me…" and I would think, "What do I see?" and "What does this mean?"

In trusting me to receive the images and to hear their stories, and to respond, they asked me to continue my work.

Because of my readers, I wrote *Living Among Meat Eaters* and *The Pornography of Meat*.

Because of my readers, I created *The Sexual Politics of Meat* slideshow.

Some of the authors of the essays in this anthology realized in reading *The Sexual Politics of Meat* that they weren't alone. During some of the years of the 1980s, writing *The Sexual Politics of Meat* was a lonely time for me. As the book went out into the world, I learned that I, too, wasn't alone.

Out of loneliness came community. And some of the best damn vegan meals one could possibly imagine. (In fact, I don't need to imagine them anymore because talented vegan chefs are creating them.)

Many readers write to tell me that because of *The Sexual Politics of Meat* they became vegan. I understand; writing it had that effect on me, too.

I devoted a chapter of *The Sexual Politics of Meat* to examining the history of influence—how someone encounters a vegetarian text and, inspired by it, becomes a vegetarian. I wrote, "Vegetarianism is often parented, to a large degree, by books."

Did I hope my feminist-vegan book would be such a parent? I don't remember! But if I had, I am sure I would have wanted to imagine that any daughters would be defiant, would insist on putting their own interpretation on my words.

Resistance is beautiful. Resistance is powerful. Resistance is found in the pages of this book. I am thrilled by the way another generation moves all this forward.

I marvel at what a gift I am continually given—to be the author of a book that matters to others and to meet wonderful individuals, hear their visions, and be included in justice-seeking communities around the world.

By the writers who contributed to this book, I am humbled and honored and amazed. I am thankful for each of them and for Mia MacDonald of Brighter Green for conceiving the book, Martin Rowe for moving it forward, and Kara Davis and Wendy Lee for overseeing this fascinating collection of essays. Some of the women represented here I have been lucky enough to meet and some I can hardly wait to meet.

At the end of *The Sexual Politics of Meat*, I quote from a lovely poem by Virginia de Araújo. She describes a friend who takes the barrenness of a cupboard, filled only with "celery threads, chard stems, avocado skins" and creates a vegan feast and says "on this grace I feed."

What she has in the kitchen is not what I think of as abundant vegan living, but in these pages we have defiant daughters recreating the world with a vision of abundance.

This generation isn't going to settle for "celery threads, chard stems, avocado skins." Why should they? They've got their own vision, have created their own recipes, will teach us things we did not know we needed to know, and will continue to make important, vital connections.

And on this grace may we all feed.

Carol J. Adams

Dallas, Texas

12/12/12

Cow

Halal

RUBY HAMAD

My vegetarianism had very little to do with my feminism, or so I thought.

I was what could accurately be described as a "feminist" long before I even knew what one was, certainly before I had even heard of the term. Growing up on the tail end of a family of seven children in 1980s Australia I had, as a small child, what seemed like unlimited freedom. My Arab Muslim parents made very little, if any, differentiation between my younger brother and me.

I was a tomboy. While my older sisters were called in to scrub floors, wash dishes, and gut fish with my mother, I was sure to be found outdoors with my only younger sibling. If we weren't climbing trees, we would be playing hide-and-seek on the rooftop of our primary school, engrossed in a game of backyard cricket, or doing backflips at the local swimming pool.

Gender did not come between us. Not in our early years. We were equals. The Sydney summers seemed endless. Life was good—until puberty hit. That's when the illusion of equality was shattered.

I first noticed it at about the age of eleven. Whereas before, my brother and I would loiter around the playground hanging off the monkey bars until it started to get dark, my mother began demanding I come directly home after school. The pleas for permission to play a game of touch football with the neighborhood kids (mostly boys) were treated with openmouthed expressions of horror.

You want to play with the boys?

By the time I was twelve, I too was being saddled with chores. The chore I hated most, the one that had me seething with unspoken rage, was the task of making the bed of my younger brother.

No longer my equal.

But it really hit home when I was thirteen. One of our favorite things to do every summer was to go cliff-jumping at Wattamolla, an ancient lagoon in the Royal National Park in Sydney's southern area. The seven-meter cliff rises irresistibly over the horseshoe-shaped body of water and it was not uncommon for us to spend up to an hour gathering up the courage to take the leap.

My sister and I were among the few girls who took the thrilling challenge. For many summers we happily jumped from the cliffs, hearts racing. My mother, not a fan of picnics, was usually absent and so we went with our father and our cousins. On this particular occasion our mother had tagged along. Patriarchy needs the participation of both women and men in order to perpetuate itself, and my mother's brand of collusion was more active than most. The sight of her two youngest, virginal daughters jumping off the cliff edge and landing in the water with an almighty splash almost sent her into an apoplectic fit.

First let me say that, being Muslim, our parents never did have "that" talk with us. So even though my sister and I were both teenagers who knew about sex (at least we knew that people "did it"), our mother tried to convey her alarm at our bodies hitting the water at great speeds, without actually telling us why.

Girls shouldn't jump off cliffs.

Why not? All the boys are doing it.

She sniffed at our retort. Now, my mother has never heard of Joe Jackson but her next words echoed his exactly (albeit in an entirely different language, since she spoke only Arabic):

Don't you know that it's different for girls?

Her cryptic language was too much for me. I had no clue what she was talking about. My sister had to explain to me later that our mother freaked out because she thought the force of the water would break our hymens.

That's when I knew.

I knew that the gap between how my brothers were treated and how my sisters and I were treated was only going to grow, and that the reason was our girl bodies. I knew that my days of freedom were numbered. And I knew I wasn't going to tolerate it.

I wasn't the rebellious type, at least, not overtly. My rebellion took place entirely within my own mind: at the age of thirteen I determined that I wasn't going to put up with this forever. I made up my mind that I would accept my parents' control over my body only until I was old enough to legally take matters into my own hands. *As soon as I turn eighteen*, I vowed to myself, *I'm outta here.*

In many ways, I was a dutiful daughter. Because I never exhibited any outward signs of discontent, it would be an understatement to say that my parents were caught by surprise when, at the age of nineteen and unmarried, I left the house one morning and never came back. It certainly never occurred to them—it did not occur to me until decades later—that the signs of my rebelliousness were there. They had simply missed them. Had they been paying closer attention they would have seen me question patriarchal authority from as far back as the age of five.

For it was at this age that I began showing signs of a deep discomfort with the practice of eating meat.

IT ALL STARTED with a chicken. I am often saddened at the inability of many adults to recall just how much children view animals as equals. At the age of five, I was thrilled to wander in to the backyard one day and find a chicken scratching away in the garden. She seemed to come out of nowhere and I didn't think to ask what she was doing there because there she was and that was good enough for me. I quickly informed her she was my new best friend and immediately set about chasing her all over the yard. So it struck my five-year-old self as nothing short of tragic to see myself go, a few short days later, from trying to settle on a name for her to witnessing my father hold her fragile body in his big hands and, invoking the name of God, slice her little head clean off her neck. Yes, it's true. Headless chickens really do run around like . . . headless chickens.

I was too shocked to scream. Instead, I fled to the garage, which had been her short-lived home, and lay there trembling for hours, curled among the straw and her stray feathers. My parents thought my devastation was sweet but entirely unnecessary. It never crossed their minds that I was grieving the loss of my best friend.

That was my first brush with the patriarchal model of meat consumption. I didn't know it then, but eating meat is, in its very nature, an expression of male power and control over the bodies of others. There is no denying this now. We are all, vegetarian and meat eater alike, aware of how closely aligned eating meat is with the stereotypical notion of "masculinity." I remember the Australian advertising campaigns of the 1980s urging housewives to "Feed the man meat!"

In the case of my doomed childhood pet, well, just picture it: A

helpless bird finds herself at the mercy of the power of the father—
my father—who in turn looks to the heavenly father (although Muslims do not refer to God as "Father," they do follow the familiar woman-man-God hierarchy), for permission and justification in the taking of the chicken's life. Killing and eating animals is considered part of the natural order. This, of course, is the same order that places men above women. It is the same order that proscribes rigid gender roles to which we are expected to conform. *Don't you know that it's different for girls?*

I didn't eat that chicken. And though I would like to say I never ate chicken or any other dead animal again, the dominant culture that sanctions meat as normal, natural, and necessary is a tough force to defy and, in time, I forgot the pain.

My grief, however, reignited a decade later when, as a fifteen-year-old, I witnessed a grainy home video of relatives in Syria slaughtering a sheep after a death in the family. The animal sacrifice is a long-standing religious tradition, with the meat to be distributed among the poor. I, however, couldn't reconcile the blood rushing from the animal's limp body with the concept of "charity." The life draining from the sheep synchronized with the innocence draining from my soul. This is when I announced my intention to go vegetarian for the first time, a declaration that was met with a mixture of amusement and horror by my Muslim parents: *But God made animals for us to eat!*

Vegetarianism, while not exactly unheard of, is certainly rare in a religion that sanctions meat as halal—permissible—provided it comes from the "right" animal (i.e., not pork—but more on that later). My decision to turn against the practice of meat eating came two years after my silent resolve to leave my religion as soon as I came of age.

Was this a coincidence? At that stage, I thought so. I had no way of making the connection. I didn't think I was being a "feminist" by refusing to accept my place in the natural order of things. I only knew I wanted to be free. And I thought that not wanting to eat meat had nothing to do with my resolve to live an autonomous life. Now I can appreciate that what I was rebelling against, both on my own behalf and that of animals, was that it is acceptable and natural for some to control and dominate others.

In an attempt to nip my vegetarianism in the bud, my mother refused to cook separate meals for my benefit. Like in most cultures, food and the symbolism that surround it is a huge part of part of daily Muslim life, with women often spending the best part of the day preparing the main meal. Eating together was one of the few things we did as a family and was not a matter taken lightly by my parents. Fortunately Middle Eastern food contains many meat-free dishes, so some days I didn't feel challenged at all. On the days my mother did cook a meat-based dish I tried to make do with frozen spinach, peas, and corn on the cob. This was particularly hard on the weekends when my married brothers and sisters visited and the table would be laid out with a seemingly endless variety of beautifully seasoned dishes. As my parents knew I would, I soon tired of my self-imposed exile from the family bonding sessions and I once again ate what was put in front of me.

Eventually, I began to enjoy it.

The rest of my years at home continued in this pattern of vowing to stop eating meat but being unable to do so. In Arab culture (whether within the Middle East or throughout the diaspora) it is extremely rare for young women to move away from home before their wedding day. It was such an excruciating decision for me that I missed my own deadline and didn't gather the courage to leave until a few weeks shy of my twentieth birthday. It's not an easy thing to know you are responsible for suffering in others. In my parents' case, it was both pain at losing their daughter and humiliation at being the subject of malicious community gossip.

And then a funny thing happened. Within three weeks of leaving home I stopped eating red meat. A few weeks after that and chicken and fish also disappeared from my diet. What I had tried and failed at for so many years growing up ended up being one of the easiest things I have ever done.

The process was made somewhat easier due to my rather major problem with pork. It's hard to convey how deep the aversion is that Muslims have to pork. *The Muslim World League Journal* says:

> The pig is naturally lazy and indulgent in sex, it is dirty, greedy and gluttonous. It dislikes sunlight and lacks the spirit and will to "fight." It eats almost anything, be it human excreta or anything foul . . . you may feed the pig on clean, wholesome food, but you can't change its nature. It is still a pig and will always stay so.

Yes, that's right, the aversion runs so deep, is so visceral, that not only is the flesh regarded as contaminated but even the character of the pig becomes a potential moral contagion to humans.

This aversion was instilled into me as a child. In our childhood games, if we truly wanted to hurt each other, it wasn't with sticks or stones, or slaps or punches. We would simply call each other the worst slur we could think of: *Pig!*

Becoming a vegetarian wasn't at the forefront of my mind in those first few weeks out of home. I had learned to ignore the voice in my head telling me I was participating in something intrinsically wrong every time I put part of a dead animal in my mouth. However, given the taboo instilled from earliest childhood, I knew there was no way I could overcome my aversion to any form of pig meat. At the same time, I knew that eating other animals while abstaining from pork, even in the absence of religious belief, didn't make sense. As much as pork is forbidden and reviled in Islamic culture, it is sanctioned and embraced in the Western culture that I so desperately wanted to be a part of.

I didn't realize at the time that my dilemma cut to the heart of the dominant order that Carol Adams spends much of *The Sexual Politics of Meat* critiquing. My internal conflict with what Adams terms my "personal taboos" overtly questioned the arbitrary relationship humans have with animals. I couldn't answer that eternal question: *Why is it natural to eat some animals and not others?* In the end, I decided it would be much simpler to avoid the issue altogether and do what I had always wanted to do—become a vegetarian.

Just like that, my meat-eating days were behind me.

AND SO I had two equally important threads running throughout my life. My feminism and vegetarianism were each important to me in their own way, but I saw them as unrelated aspects of myself. The process toward reconciliation of these two vital parts of me began when I made the transition from vegetarian to vegan more than a year ago. This time the catalyst was witnessing some particularly graphic footage of the slaughtering of cattle that had been exported from Australia to Indonesia.

Australia has a thriving live animal export industry. Every year four million sheep and cattle are sent on long, perilous trips to (mainly Muslim) markets as close as Indonesia and as far as Egypt and Turkey. Many do not survive the journey. In 2011, animal advocacy group Animals Australia conducted an undercover investigation into the Indonesian market. What they found led campaign director Lyn White to declare she believed they had shot enough material within the first five minutes to shut the industry down for good.

The footage, aired on the Australian Broadcasting Association's prime time current affairs program *Four Corners*, caused unprecedented outrage. Across the country, petitions were signed, politicians were emailed, and rallies were attended, as people demanded an end to live exports.

Like many Australians I, too, was outraged. Unlike many Australians my anger wasn't directed primarily at the Indonesians. The general public consensus was fury at "their" treatment of "our" cattle. The desire to lay blame sparked widespread anti-Muslim sentiment due to halal ritual slaughter practices requiring animals to be conscious at the time of slaughter. The large animals died a slow, torturous death in chronically ill-staffed and ill-equipped abattoirs. Many of them suffered up to twenty minutes of torture: having their tails broken, their tendons slashed, fingers poked in their eyes, feet kicking them in the head, and water hoses sprayed directly up their nostrils. Still the end wouldn't come; all this was followed by clumsily repeated jabs to the throat with dull knives.

Every step of the way, these gentle creatures never stopped fighting. They shook in fear as they witnessed others being cut up in front of their eyes. They bellowed in protest. They resisted. They tried to escape. *They wanted to live.* The animals suffered mentally as well as physically; there is no doubt about that. One of the doomed steers (posthumously named "Tommy" by Animals Australia) can clearly be seen shaking, his heart beating almost out of his chest as he witnessed another steer killed and dismembered before his eyes. He knew he was next.

I do not believe blaming Muslim culture itself addresses the real issue of why these animals suffered so greatly. Such shocking treatment of farmed animals is not something particular to Indonesia or Islam, but is an example of the impossibility of meeting even the most basic welfare guidelines when animals are treated as things rather than as beings. A recent New South Wales government review found breaches in all ten of that state's abattoirs that process red meat. When 100 percent of abattoirs cannot meet welfare standards, one could argue that animal cruelty is less an aberration in the industry and more of a business model.

At the time I saw the video, despite my youthful claims never to return, I was living with my mother who, after a life spent raising seven children, unexpectedly found herself alone following the sudden death of my younger brother. My father had passed on six years earlier. Reconnecting with my roots after so many years, it was startling to find myself immersed in a language, culture, and religion to which I had barely given a passing thought for well over a decade. This time I was able to consider it more objectively, from the viewpoint of someone who could leave at any time rather than be forced to submit to its every tenet. This allowed me to consider the live export saga from both a Western and Muslim perspective.

As I struggled to make sense of the gruesome images, I recalled how, after my hen's death, my father had attempted to console me. God, he said, had made it halal (permissible) to eat animals but only as long as the animal was killed quickly without prolonged suffering. And it is true that the death of my hen at his hands had at least been mercifully swift.

Halal slaughter actually proscribes strict conditions designed to minimize animal distress. The knife must be clean and razor sharp. The animal must be killed with one quick stroke. Animals must not be bound, provoked, or beaten. They must not be killed within sight of each other and they must not be made to wait. "If you must kill," the Prophet Mohammed said, "kill without torture." Contrary to popular belief, "stunning"—rendering an animal temporarily unconscious immediately prior to slaughter—is not prohibited in Islam, and is in fact widely practiced in Islamic abattoirs throughout the world. The requirement that animals be slaughtered conscious was, in Mohammed's time, simply mandated for health reasons to ensure the animal wasn't already dead.

Clearly, every single of these conditions were being flaunted in Indonesia. But if Islam itself wasn't to blame, then what was? The answer lies in the footage itself. Just like in Australian slaughterhouses, the animals come faster than they can be killed. Workers are undertrained and overworked. Many of the men are young (some just teenagers) and slight, battling Australian cattle that weigh 600+ kilograms. It is clear that the torture meted out to the cows was not sadistic but the actions of tired, frustrated men who were desperate to do something, anything, to make the animal comply.

The problem is systematic and endemic. When the goal is to kill as many animals in as short a time as possible—which is the goal wherever animals are killed commercially—then there is little room for concern for that animal's welfare. By blaming Islam itself, Australians were saved the trouble of seeing themselves reflected in that footage. Suddenly, "stunning" became the hallmark of humane treatment of animals. We stun and they don't. We eat animals the "right" way. We are good. They are bad. They don't deserve our cows.

I saw myself in that footage. I saw the self that, despite not having eaten meat for well over a decade, still provided meat to my crew on my film school sets. I saw the self that occasionally ate eggs and cheese all the while silencing the voice in my head telling me that animals suffer for these, too. And I saw the self that once felt as trapped as those cows and yearned to be free. I saw myself in the slaughter-men and I saw myself in the cows.

I resolved never to be associated with animal abuse and exploitation ever again. I had been toying with the idea of phasing all animal products from my diet since reading about the routine forced separation of cows and their baby calves in the dairy industry, but this video turned me into a practicing vegan literally overnight.

And yet I made the transition to veganism based on my empathy with the cattle, not quite realizing the link between patriarchy and animal exploitation. I still thought of these as different issues. It was thus with a heavy heart that I picked up *The Sexual Politics of Meat* a few weeks later. I was feeling as though my feminism were burnt out. More accurately, I felt it had been snuffed out by my sudden, all-consuming passion for animal justice.

As a writer I had focused primarily on overtly feminist issues, including gender representation in popular culture, the treatment of women in the Arab world, and the virgin-whore dichotomy. Despite having been a vegetarian for the whole of my adulthood, I managed to convince myself that animal rights is a "lesser" issue, one that we could get to after we had solved all the problems plaguing humanity. Why waste time trying to get people to care about the suffering of other species when so many barely seemed moved by the suffering of our own?

Witnessing the futile struggle of those doomed cows on video, and the look of utter confusion on their faces, I realized how wrong I was. I knew I would never be able to view the world the same way again. I was aghast that, unlike women's oppression, animal abuse was something in which almost all of us are complicit. I wanted—needed—to spread the word of animal advocacy, but I feared this would have to come at the expense of my feminism. After all, animal rights and women's rights had to compete for space in the public consciousness. Moreover, given the shock tactics of groups like PETA who aren't averse to exploiting the female body in order to sell their animal rights message, the two are not only unrelated but even adversarial, I reasoned.

It was in an effort to answer this question that I turned to the book *The Sexual Politics of Meat.*

And there it was. The link between my feminism and my vegetarianism. My early feminism and attempts at vegetarianism were a challenge to this culture in which humans treat animals the way patriarchy treats women. The reason meat made me uncomfortable as a child was because it was a reminder of my own powerlessness. Much like women, animals suffer because they are treated as commodities. Relegated to the status of objects, their own desires are irrelevant. They simply exist to be used and abused. This is not specific to one culture or religion; it is a global, structural problem that stems from the belief that the powerful have the right to dominate the weak.

Feminists who eat meat may be fighting for their own liberation, but as long as they participate in animal exploitation—*Feed the man meat!*—they are propping up the very system they are fighting against.

I WENT BACK over my life, reassessing my relationship with my parents, my cultural background, feminism, and my attitudes to meat. In the book, Carol Adams writes, "Vegetarianism is a conscious decision that permeates every aspect of life." I would add, "So, too, is feminism." It was my feminism that propelled me to turn my back on thousands of years of culture, which in turn gave me the opportunity to turn my back on meat consumption. Would I ever have stopped eating animals had I remained at home and married a good Muslim boy, for whom I would have been expected to cook meat? I don't know what might have been, but what I do know is that once my decision was made, there has not being a moment's regret, no temptation, no second thoughts.

Halal or not, there was simply no other way for me to be.

My early rejection of patriarchal authority and my repeated attempts at living a meat-free life were indeed related. I was rejecting control over both my body and the bodies of animals with whom I have always identified. I am a feminist and a vegan because I am opposed to all oppression, to all violence, to all discrimination. I am opposed to the so-called "natural order" that regards perceived inferiority as permission to deny basic rights.

It was not so long ago that women and blacks were deemed soulless and said to lack sufficient intellect to deserve autonomy. Baby animals continue to be taken away from their mothers with the same reassurances given when black women in America and indigenous women in Australia suffered the same abuse. *They don't love them like us. They won't remember them like us. They are not us.*

But, indeed, they are like us. I knew that as a five-year-old when I shed tears over a hen who died before I could even give her a name. This revelation has permeated my work in which I urge my fellow feminists not to ignore the links between feminism and veganism. We must examine our own human privilege the way we examine male privilege and race privilege and class privilege. As women, we should see ourselves reflected in the suffering of animals, because as Adams reminds us, we are the ones who "have been swallowed *and* we are the swallowers. We are the consumers *and* the consumed."

It's not just my professional life that has been altered. My personal life appears to have come almost full circle. Leaving my family gave me the freedom to adopt my vegetarian lifestyle. Reconciling with my mother well over a decade later, I finally came to understand why I became a vegetarian in the first place, why I have always identified with animals.

As vegan feminists, our best weapons in our fight for a fairer world are ourselves. I once thought the differences between myself and my family were insurmountable, that we would never be part of each other's lives again. But time and grief can make even the most significant differences seem negligible. When my brother died without warning, I found myself nursing my mother through an unbearable loss. The proverbial prodigal daughter, I became part of the family again, but this time on my own terms, and to her credit, not once has my mother tried to change me.

My family still bonds over food. I have been fortunate enough to attend many of these recent gatherings. The intrinsic distress I feel when witnessing people eating meat aside, I enjoy them in a way I never did as a child, the way you enjoy doing something because you want to, not because you have to. Nowadays, among all the meat there is sure to be at least one vegan dish served in my honor, a respect for my choice that I didn't get as a teenager.

A few weeks ago, we were at the home of my oldest brother, who is very traditional. The whole family was there—my mother, my siblings, their partners, and their children. I cast my eyes over the dinner table; there were at least three types of salad and two types of kibbeh. And then it struck me. Out of all of these dishes that my meat-eating sister-in-law had painstakingly prepared, only one of them contained meat. The rest were entirely vegan. It was a small symbol, a tiny step, but one that gives me hope that my life's work may not be in vain.

A Moment of Truth

ROCHELLE M. GREEN

$\mathcal{A}$s a philosophy professor, I've had many experiences with students that define my purpose as a teacher. I regularly teach courses in feminist philosophy, social political philosophy, race theory, and environmental philosophy that invite political dialogue about personal experiences and choices. Due to their subject matter, these courses carry with them responsibilities toward students that may not necessarily accompany other sorts of classes. It is not uncommon for a student to contact me about experiences of sexism or homophobia after taking my feminist philosophy class. Sometimes, a student will have had firsthand experience with domestic abuse. In my philosophy of race class, students often find themselves thinking about ways they've been a part of institutions that maintained racist practices. Other students will contend with hearing their classmates ask questions that reveal an ignorance about what it feels like to be a member of an oppressed group. In all of these cases, I have to figure out how to best help students through these experiences and maintain a safe but challenging learning environment.

For example, one day S., a female undergraduate, stopped by my office during office hours. As I sat at my desk working at the computer, I could just barely hear her tentative knock on the door. This struck me as odd, primarily because S. was a popular student around our department and was a usual visitor to office hours. Typically, she would either knock or announce herself with far more self-confidence. I had a sense something was wrong.

"Come on in," I said.

Slowly opening the door, she said in a whisper, "Can I speak with you?"

The trembling in her voice alarmed me. I realized something wasn't just wrong, S. was not herself. She was visibly nervous and clearly distressed. I thought I detected tears pooling in her eyes, but she fought them back. I motioned for her to sit down and nodded at the door as if to say, "You can close it you like," which she did. I moved a box of tissues closer to her and quietly asked her how I might help.

"Something happened the other night. I'm really confused about it," she said.

"Do you want to tell me about it?"

"Well . . . A friend and I went to a party and there was quite a bit of drinking. You know?" She sniffled a little bit, her voice still unsure. "Well, my friend's really upset and I think she may have been raped, but I don't really know for sure. She's telling everyone that she just hooked up, but she doesn't seem okay to me."

Without thinking, I mumbled a few words about how college parties are prime contexts for sexual assault and rape and that if S. thought something happened, it's likely to be the case that something did actually happen. As I pressed for further information, S. became increasingly nervous, and I became increasingly concerned that she wasn't really telling me the whole story. Nevertheless, I continued asking questions about her friend.

"Does your friend have someone she can talk with? Where is she now?"

"Oh, she's okay for now. She said she wasn't feeling well and isn't going to class today, so I think she'll be all right. I really just want to know what I should tell her. If a girl gets really drunk at a party and doesn't want to have sex, she shouldn't have to, right? Even if she's drunk?"

I leaned in, over the desk. "It doesn't matter if she was drunk. It doesn't matter if she stripped. No one should have forced her to do anything she didn't want to do under any circumstances."

"Well, in this case, this guy kept following her around the party and grabbing her. I could tell she didn't really want him to, but she kept sort of smiling and telling other people that he just really liked her. As everyone was leaving, he stayed. I saw her telling people, kind of joking, that he was trying to spend the night and she didn't want him to. Then the last group of guys were left and she asked them to stay a while longer, which they did, but it got so late. Anyway, the guys got the hint and tried to walk this other guy out of the house to his car, but I guess he didn't really leave. He ended up going back into the house and my friend said she was so drunk she couldn't really stop him. Anyway, that's rape, right? I mean, if my friend tried to get him to leave and he didn't, it's rape, right?"

I realized as I listened to her story that certain details seemed to be missing and others seemed so certain. I began to suspect that S. was really talking about herself. The tone in her voice, the urgency with which she was asking me these questions, made it personal. I assured her over and over again that "her friend" did nothing wrong, and that she wasn't responsible, however drunk or incapacitated she was. I tried to soothe her, explaining that "her friend" clearly wasn't comfortable with the situation because she had tried to alert so many people to her discomfort.

We continued to talk like this for quite some time. It became fairly clear S. was talking about herself and that she had actually been the one hosting the party. I tried again and again without success to lessen her pain. The best I could offer was the time and space for her to speak and the refuge of a measly, overcrowded office. Listening to her, though, I heard her message loud and clear. This scared, vulnerable woman was identifying herself as the meat receptacle. She had been objectified, fragmented, and consumed. I feared for her because I saw in her face, in her expressions, that she had already begun the process of internalizing the guilt, of blaming herself, and of detaching from her own humanity.

After that first conversation, S. began stopping by my office more frequently. She began distancing herself from many of her peers, and I began to hear from other professors that her attendance, which had been perfect, was slipping as well. Nevertheless, she managed to come to my office a few times a week, usually around lunchtime. I had the impression that my office had become a place where she could hide from other people's well-intentioned inquiries about her suddenly detached demeanor. Sometimes I'd hear other students urging her to go out with them and kindly ribbing her for declining. She clearly had not discussed her experience nor her feelings with them. She was also beginning to lose weight. Her face seemed pale, gaunt. She was struggling.

This became all the more clear to me when she began bringing food to our meetings. As she did, she began to tell me how she hadn't been eating. With a rather sardonic laugh, she added, "But then I got this craving for a good old-fashioned hamburger, so here I am! I guess I won't be starving after all!"

It was hard to accept this change in her behavior. S. had been vegan for five years, something I'd learned in the feminist philosophy course I'd taught the year before. I felt the hamburger was yet another symbol of her self-loathing. When I broached the subject with her, inquiring about her sudden shift to meat eating, she claimed she didn't care about the issue anymore. Although she confessed that eating animal foods had made her feel quite sick at first, she added, "At least I know I can still feel something."

I realized S.'s struggle was one identified in *The Sexual Politics of Meat*. She was consuming the absent referent in much the same way she, as the absent referent, had also been consumed. She wasn't only at the front of the battle between women and patriarchy, she literally *was* that front. She was enacting the wrong done to her on other beings as a means of trying to regain agency.

I FIRST READ *The Sexual Politics of Meat* as a senior in college. I was part of a feminist organization that regularly participated in academic and extracurricular activities on campus. We organized events like Take Back the Night and showcased women musicians for the student programs during Women's History Month. Several of us also worked as student organizers and presenters at a regional women's studies conference each year. Being a member of this group exposed me to new ideas about politics: it was within this context I first encountered Marx, first started thinking through the political implications of homosexuality, and first met women of color who were critical of the standard white, middle-class, American feminism I'd learned about in classes.

As I read Adams' book, I was really just beginning to question gender roles and scripts in my own experiences. Though I realized the extent to which I was complicit in oppressive practices of the dominant culture, I wasn't quite ready to change. Regardless of how interesting or intuitive the ideas in this book were, I was not yet ready to critique myself. Before I could really internalize Adams' point, I needed to come to terms with the variety of ways in which I participated in my own oppression by accepting aspects of patriarchal culture. At the time, I wasn't sure I wanted to be a wife and a mother, but I certainly knew I wanted to be self-determined and equal to my male peers. What was incredibly confusing to me was the way in which I saw women seemingly "having it all" by playing up their expected feminine roles, or women gaining power through their sexuality.

This was especially pernicious in my philosophy courses. Often there would only be one or two women in the class, myself included. Several of the women students would regularly flirt with professors and other students alike, often using class discussions as a context for showcasing the various ways in which feminine intelligence can be rendered more palatable to men. They would dress provocatively and behave in ways suggesting that their contributions to the field of philosophy were secondary to those of their male counterparts. To my young mind, these seemed like blatant contradictory messages: on the one hand, feminism was telling me that I need not seek shelter in stereotypical gender scripting, and on the other hand, it seemed as if my cultural milieu was suggesting that to embrace such scripting was precisely how one got ahead as a woman.

I was also being exposed to the prevalence of sexual violence for the first time. While living on campus, I learned that several of my dorm mates had been sexually assaulted. Whenever I experienced unwanted advances from male classmates, I shrugged them off while trying to simultaneously shirk the feeling that there was something inherently wrong with my body, with my female being. Between all the blue safety phones scattered across campus and the rape hotline numbers listed on the backs of bathroom stall doors, I became acutely aware of the connection between women's sexuality and violence. This was an uneasy realization for me; it made me feel *like a piece of meat.* I had to somehow reconcile myself to the fact that I could be the site of violence, the object of violence.

Years later, my attempts to help S. gain control of her life again made me recognize what I had failed to see in my own college experiences. Now I could see how participation in oppressive practices, like the consumption of animal products, masks the distress we feel as absent referents ourselves.

S. continued to visit me regularly during my office hours. My office became a safe space for her when she was on campus. She was such a frequent visitor, I ended up putting a little student desk in a common room close to my office where she could have some privacy while she studied. She continued her practice of bringing lunch to my office, and her lunches continued to involve meat products. One day in the spring semester, I resolved myself to ask her about the meat again.

"So," I said, "have you decided to give up your vegetarianism completely?"

She replied in a rather offhanded way, "I don't really think about it that much." She looked at the bookshelves instead of me. I realized she might not have fully processed what her meat eating meant because of the way she seemed both dismissive and defensive when I inquired further.

"You were an avid vegan a few months ago. Has something changed your perspective about the more-than-human-world?"

She replied more straightforwardly, "No, nothing has really

changed my views. I just got tired to trying to fight everything. I guess it's just easier to eat meat. Besides, I've been careful lately only to get meat that is sustainably raised and organic."

I found her last statement ironic. A year before, S. was charging other students with unthinking conformity when they said similar things in response to her critique of American meat consumption. I decided not to push the issue further with her that day and instead began asking her questions about her friends and her social circle. I knew this was a touchy subject since S. had distanced herself from most of her peers.

She hesitated a bit and after quite a long silence responded by telling me that she'd tried to talk to one of them about her rape.

"A while ago I tried to explain what happened to B. I figured that since she's always identified herself as such a strong feminist, she would be able to help me and would understand what happened."

S. paused and then continued with her story.

"She didn't believe me. I told her all about the party and everything and she just didn't believe me. B. knows who the guy is and says he's a good person and that I probably misunderstood what happened. She just doesn't believe me."

I sat, stunned, as I listened to her. I watched as she grew more visibly upset, trying to tell me about her betrayal by someone she thought was not only a friend, but a fellow feminist as well. Again, I was left searching for the right words.

"Acquaintance rapes are the most common types of rape," I said. "Part of what makes them so difficult to report is that everyone knows the people involved. I won't defend B.'s response, but it isn't uncommon for people to respond this way to these kinds of situations."

S. nodded along. I knew that she intellectually understood this, but it was clear that she couldn't feel it. In fact, her experience had essentially undermined most of what she knew intellectually about these kinds of issues.

"How did it make you feel when B. defended him?" I asked.

"I just felt betrayed. I still feel betrayed. I don't understand how someone can call themselves a feminist and then act like that. Ever since I've known her, B. has always made a big deal about sexism and now here's an actual problem and she doesn't help me!" S. was clearly angry.

"Did you ever try to tell anyone else?"

"No," S. answered, "I can't. I don't want to anymore. I just don't think people understand what I've been through. And they especially don't see how they've made it worse!"

After this conversation with S., I began to better understand her tendency to isolate herself as well as her return to animal foods. She had not only experienced the heartbreak of the loss of a friend, she was experiencing the loss of her ideals as well. As I thought of how to help her, it occurred to me that she might benefit from further exposure to people like her and to people who regularly followed through on their political commitments. I decided to incorporate sections of the book *The Sexual Politics of Meat* into an ethics course I knew she was planning on taking the following semester. I had asked S. about the book before and knew she had already read it, but I hoped it would help her remember the importance of political movements and perhaps restore her faith in the possibility for solidarity.

At the beginning of the ethics class, S. commented to me that she was happy to see the text on the syllabus, and as we approached that unit in the course, she seemed to be back in form. She wasn't as vocal as she had been previously, but she was definitely invested in the discussion. The class as a whole discussed a number of issues, including whether or not it was fair to compare the oppression of women to the oppression of animals. This group of students was quick to understand the link and, though a few people continued to critically question the association, most of the members of the class responded with strong arguments and carefully reasoned questions. As I watched S. work through the material, it was as if she was working through her trauma again, but in a new and different way. Slowly, I noticed the meat disappearing again from her lunches. I never asked her about her meat-eating again.

Today S. is active in women's grassroots organizing. She finished her degree and began working for a nonprofit in her hometown. We are still in touch and she is still a vegan. Today, she credits *The Sexual Politics of Meat* with her return to her feminist principles.

As for me, I continue my own feminist vegetarian quest. I take with me to each class the recognition that students will approach learning about oppression in a variety of ways. I try to remain cognizant of the situations they face on a regular basis and to be sensitive to the ways in which acknowledging what is right might be challenging. I try to cultivate safe spaces for students to work through new political ideas and perspectives. In the end, *The Sexual Politics of Meat* is a story about how we are all implicated and capable of challenging our own complicity in a system of oppression. Just as S. was able to reevaluate her own responses to sexualized violence, every one of us can reevaluate our relationship to the texts of meat.

Names and identifying details have been changed
to protect the privacy of those involved.

The Sexual Politics of Breastfeeding

JENNIFER GRUBBS

 *I*t is 9:00 A.M. and I have two and a half hours until my daughter needs to breastfeed again. Earlier this year I gave birth to a beautiful baby and entered the world of motherhood. As an anarchafeminist, vegan, and now a mother, I know there will be many challenges to raising a daughter within a world that is overly capitalist, heteropatriarchal (power structured around male-dominated ideals), and violently speciesist (the systematic privileging of one species over others).

My partner and I, both doctoral students in the Washington, D.C. area, spent the forty weeks of pregnancy doing what we knew best—research. The tasks immediately piled up: find a midwifery practice, find a doula, make dietary adjustments (more green smoothies), take childbirth classes, take a hospital tour, find a pediatrician, and so on. But these were just the logistics. In preparation for motherhood I imagined countless hypothetical scenarios about raising a child and tried to envision how I would handle them. How do I tell my daughter about the violence of patriarchy, authoritarianism, speciesism, and capitalism? How do I prepare her for a world that is systematically unkind? How do I ensure that she will disrupt these systems rather than reproduce them? Family and friends attempted to ease my concerns with optimism. But I turned to the mentor who helped me face the moral dilemmas of political awareness in my late teens and early twenties. I turned to Carol Adams' book *The Sexual Politics of Meat* as I attempted to rearticulate my own politics in preparation for motherhood.

My own awareness began with a book. I spent my childhood in Cincinnati, Ohio, battling the disconnect that comes with both *loving* and *eating* other-than-human animals. At eight years of age, I soaked my copy of *Charlotte's Web* in tears. I announced I wanted to stop eating meat. I was deeply disturbed by the reality that meat was flesh, and flesh meant murder. I was moved by the animals' fear of being killed in *Charlotte's Web*, but I was constrained by the language of the absent referent. The animal flesh was so absent in my referents of food that I did not identify certain foods as ground remnants of a cow. I could identify chicken wings and duck liver as animal products, but not the inconspicuous beef, burgers, and nuggets. I can remember trying to explain why eating animals felt *wrong* to me as a child. I told my family that animals experienced fear and pain, and that I did not want to be a part of that. Once I declared that I did not want to eat meat, some family members found humor in taking me to the popular Cincinnati chain, Skyline Chili, watching me eat ground beef chili without realizing that it, too, had been an animal.

Although my parents were receptive to my concern for animals, some of the usual contradictions were apparent in my family. We kept dogs as pets, served cows as meat, and wore skins as leather. When I now answer the (commonly asked) question, "When did you go vegan and why?", I share the story of when my father came home saying he had bought a calf. For months I would ask about the calf and was shown a Polaroid of it living on a farm. One day, my father returned home and said he had brought the cow with him. I eagerly ran to the front door, expecting to see the cow in the front lawn. To my dismay, it was not there. "It is in my trunk, Jennifer," my father said. I remember pausing with confusion, and then realizing what he meant. For my father, this was an attempt for his children living in a Cincinnati suburb to understand exactly where our meat came from.

In the years that followed, I received little support from family, my pediatrician, or school friends, and I knew no other vegetarians. I went back to consuming animals but I continued to express my discomfort. I went to a famous chicken joint in Cincinnati the summer of my senior year in high school and ordered their chicken tenders. I bit into a piece of chicken flesh and a vein crunched in my mouth. I immediately gagged and covered the table in vomit, then with tears. That was the last time I attempted to eat animals. I went home from the restaurant and declared I was a vegetarian. My mother, who had remained relatively indifferent as I was dragged kicking and screaming to meals of meat, also decided to go vegetarian that evening. I attended meetings with animal rights groups, read guides to vegetarianism, and watched documentaries that detailed the exploitation of animals in various industries. Two years after going veg, I was an outspoken vegan advocate.

The second time around was different. Although family and friends voiced questions and nutritional concerns, they did not attempt to sabotage my decision. The summer of my first year of graduate school at the University of Cincinnati I accepted an internship at Farm Sanctuary in Watkins Glen, New York. While living in the "Intern House" I found a copy of Carol Adams' *Living Among Meat Eaters*. At the time, I identified as a feminist, as a vegan, and as an anarchist. But the book provided an analytical bridge to connect these disparate identities I struggled to balance. By the end of the six-week internship I had also read *The Sexual Politics of Meat* and *The Pornography of Meat*. From there, I used the bibliographies to find other authors and books on similar topics. Each text provided a new lens to analyze the world, and a sense of comfort knowing that I was not alone in my thoughts.

In the process of obtaining two master's degrees and a doctorate, I've written on the ways in which female bodies are commodified as mechanisms of reproduction. I've presented conference papers that interrogate the naturalization of gender roles through tropes of reproduction. I've made connections between the exploitation of women and animals within heteropatriarchy and capitalism. But despite years of analytical thought on these subjects, *my* sexual politics of meat became real when I became pregnant. As my body became subjected to the mechanisms of reproduction, and my gender identity challenged through the divisions of labor within reproductive processes, I quickly felt like the absent referent.

As if on an assembly line, I went to prenatal appointments where I endured a series of internal examinations and blood draws. My body was measured for performance, genetically inspected for "defects," and tracked for progress. At each visit I answered survey questions, including ones about my sexual history and the legal status of my relationship. Suddenly I was another female body to be judged along a spectrum of categories. My thoughts and emotions were removed and replaced with diagnostic codes and charts. According to the data, I was merely another pregnant woman to be measured and charted.

My partner and I chose to use a midwifery practice that believes in empowerment through holistic prenatal care and births. In the first meeting with the midwives they went over dietary recommendations: plant-based proteins, grains, no processed foods, no refined flours or sugars, and multiple servings of fruits and vegetables. They told me to eat plenty of the pregnancy superfood: eggs. Although the practice promotes positive health and birthing, it was clear to me that only the health and birthing of *some* species were valued.

The meeting was full of pregnant women who rubbed their burgeoning bellies and wrote down suggestions to nurture our own fertilized eggs. I wondered if I was the only one who was thinking about the glaring hypocrisy of encouraging women to consume another species' egg to nourish the fertilized egg growing inside them. Chicken eggs, deemed the absent referent "pregnancy superfood," erase the enslavement of hens necessary to commodify *their* reproduction. The "superfood" is also a product of an industry practice within hatcheries that either suffocates or grinds male chicks deemed "waste." This contradictory logic—nourishing human pregnancy through the commodification and exploitation of another species' pregnancy—relies on the absent referent. The prenatal guidelines recommend eggs, but it erases the ways in which *all* animal beings are physically and emotionally connected to their reproduction.

My partner and I enjoyed preparing for the new baby. We took childbirth classes, prenatal yoga classes, and a hospital tour. I sought out literature that would emotionally prepare me for the journey. I turned to the Physicians Committee for Responsible Medicine and others for nutritional guidelines. I watched online videos by vegan women about how to practice holistic health during pregnancy. I created my own plan for exercise, nutrition, and supplements. I planned for the material needs of the baby by collecting clothing, equipment, and miscellaneous supplies. As weeks progressed, I followed the midwifery guidelines and drank gallons of red raspberry leaf tea to strengthen my uterus and took non-gelatin evening primrose oil capsules to ripen my cervix. I bounced on my birthing ball and must have read the castile soap bottle hundreds of times while squatting in the shower to strengthen my pelvic floor. I felt empowered in the process of pregnancy, and wanted to feel in control during labor.

But nothing can prepare you for the immense amount of love you feel when your child is born. With each push, I envisioned my daughter in my arms. After six hours of labor, Emory was born in a birthing tub at George Washington University Hospital. She was placed into my arms while still connected through her umbilical cord. My partner just looked at the both of us in awe. As Emory latched onto my breast for the first time, I felt an intense sense of pride that I was able to provide my daughter with sustaining nourishment. Through breastfeeding, I was able to calm her fears, quiet her cries, and meet her nutritional needs. Again, I felt empowered by my reproductive capacities. And it was at that moment that I began to experience the sexual politics of breastfeeding.

Women are told breastfeeding is the best way to nourish your child, but social norms dictate only a small window of acceptable breastfeeding, from the appropriate age to wean to appropriate places to feed and covers to wear in public. Within heteronormative gender portrayals of women, breasts are hypersexualized and intended for seduction. Thus, to breastfeed disrupts this orientation with breasts as sexual. Breastfeeding is accepted insofar as women privately negotiate fulfilling both socially expected roles: nurturer and sexual object. In order to compartmentalize the roles of breasts, we are expected to closet our "motherly" breast behavior in public. The logic of respectability is further perpetuated by capitalism through the selling of cruel products (dairy formula) to replace wholesome biologically consistent nutrition. But women are held to standards of respectability *and* hypersexuality. Public breastfeeding has been referred to as public indecency, deeming it a sexually deviant act.

One of the most consistent comments I get from close family and friends pertains to public breastfeeding. When I nurse in public, I often get these responses from friends: "Aren't you afraid that people will stare at your breasts in a sexual way?" and "You know, other women might not like it when you do that because you're exposing your breasts in front of their male partners." Although I feel a sense of pride when I do breastfeed without a cover in public, at times I have felt visually violated. It is a mind game to transform your understanding of what it means to have someone stare at your breasts. A year ago, I would label people's stares at my cleavage as perverse and inappropriate. Today, I am expected either to cover myself in shame or accept the gawking from others as my punishment for trying to reclaim a public space for women. Breastfeeding is a biological act to sustain the life of my daughter, but it exists in a world that sexualizes women's breasts.

Another part of the politics of breastfeeding is that women are expected to accept animal exploitation in order to care for their children. My midwives and the pediatrician discussed breastfeeding with me under the assumption that I would transition to cow's milk and dairy products by the first year. When I expressed my partner's and my decision to exclusively breastfeed during the first year, and *never* introduce animal products, my intentions were called into question. I was interrogated about vitamin, mineral, and protein sources. I thought I was done answering the ever-pesky B12 question once the baby was born. I was even told, "Don't be selfish. Your child has nutritional needs and you cannot put your politics in front of that." During a meet-and-greet appointment with a prospective pediatrician, I mentioned our commitment to veganism. The pediatrician responded with hesitancy: "We can discuss diet as she gets older. You may have to make some concessions."

As I breastfeed Emory, I attempt to balance these hypocrisies—breasts as sexual, and breasts as source of nourishment. Human female reproduction as beautiful, other-than-human animal reproduction as commodity. While I experience the beautiful bonding process of motherhood, it is violently apparent how other trans-species mothers are reproductively disempowered. I chose to become pregnant with my partner; other species are raped and inseminated as an industry standard. I balanced rest and exercise during pregnancy; other species are purchased, sold, transported, and shackled during their pregnancy. I waited until my body was ready to labor; other species have their offspring torn from their wombs out of impatience. I abstained from overloading my newborn's body with vaccinations; other species are blasted with antibiotics and growth hormones throughout infancy. I enjoyed hours of uninterrupted quiet to bond with my baby; other species are separated from their mothers and sold within twelve hours after birth. I produce breast milk for my offspring; other species are expected to produce milk for an entirely different species *instead of* their own offspring. All of the constructed processes of human motherhood are systematically denied to other-than-human animals.

Perhaps some would call my identification with other animals anthropocentric (human reproduction as the norm for all species) and essentialist (compounding reproduction with gendered-female behaviors, i.e., nurture and care), but I argue the contrary. I realize that the ways in which individuals experience reproduction is uniquely subjective. Not all female animals desire the same relationship with reproduction or offspring, but they are entitled to the opportunity to experience it without coercion. My experiences are full of subjectivities as a 27-year-old cisgender, white, able-bodied, U.S.-born, Jewish, married, post-graduate-educated, class-privileged woman. Thus pregnancy, childbirth, and child rearing are a subjective process for all species. But the level of self-determination for each pregnant species is based on different levels of autonomy. The more I address my own thoughts on these issues, the more I wonder how my daughter will articulate her own relationship to animals.

What will the journey of veganism be for Emory? She thrived in utero on my vegan diet. I blasted that little embryo with green smoothies, whole grains, and plant-based proteins. I nourished her soul with animal liberation conference presentations, Occupy demonstrations, and intellectual discussions with my partner. She has been living and breathing animal lib since she was conceived. I intend to introduce her to the intersections of speciesism at a young age. She will be aware and critical of the many privileges she will enjoy as a white, U.S.-born child. The challenges I face as a vegan mother are not how to *raise* a vegan daughter, but rather how to *ensure she will choose veganism for herself.* I want her first to see the bounty and beauty in veganism rather than the violence inherent in speciesism. I hope she learns to have kindness and compassion for all beings, and that revolution does not come from a single-politic agenda. I would love to provide a positive space at home to discuss intentional consumption. I want, I hope, and I would like—but I cannot predict the dilemmas we will face as parents. The complexities of parental politics are not a topic discussed in *What to Expect When You Are Expecting.*

So, my dilemma is this: How do I negotiate the tension of wanting to shape Emory's politics and allow her the space to pave her own path? I became a vegan in response to the exposure to animal products and fought for vegan meals at family dinners. How will I deal with Emory if she becomes adversarial about veganism? What if she demands to try animal products? What if she prefers texts like the *Sweet Valley High* books over *The Sexual Politics of Meat*? There are no answers to these questions, just time to experience them. I remain optimistic that my partner and I can teach Emory compassion and the beauty of other species. We can teach veganism as plentiful delicious food rather than as deprivation. We can teach the positive, and allow her to make her own decisions.

Pig

Confessions of a Not-Yet Vegan

DARLENE SMOOT

$\mathcal{A}$t the local animal shelter where I volunteer, most of my fellow volunteers are retirees. I work with the same group of people each week and everyone has a passion for helping the dogs that wind up in our shelter. I've briefly gotten to know my fellow volunteers, though there's never much time to chat at length. The quick and hurried exchanges we have between our duties are mostly about the dogs in our care: How can people be so callous as to dump their pets at the shelter? Please give the newest dog extra grass time, he's depressed. This stray dog is stressed and needs extra attention. Did you hear the good news that that dog got adopted?

I recently overheard a few of the volunteers discuss how they had swapped a recipe for a type of pot roast (a swap that I had not taken part in, for obvious reasons). They were marveling at how well this recipe worked and were interested in how each other's meals had turned out. They began to run down the list of volunteers who had participated in the swap. A woman's name came up and it was quickly determined that she hadn't participated because she was a vegan. My fellow volunteers conferred with one another: Does this mean she doesn't eat animals? How strange that must be! What does she eat? The discussion quickly reverted to the welfare of the dogs in our shelter and back to work we went.

Although I remained silent during this quick discussion, the irony of the situation was not lost on me. How could my fellow volunteers, who so lovingly cared for the abandoned and lost dogs of our community, be so completely dismissive of all other animals, especially those that are thought of as food? Why do we place such importance on the lives of certain animals and ignore others? How do we choose which animals to eat and which to be our companions?

Animals have always been present in my life. Most children growing up in the vast suburban sprawl of Los Angeles only have access to typical domestic pets, but I was fortunate in that we had land to house other animals. I'm using the term "land" very liberally, given that our city was mostly composed of tract homes, but our single acre was in a neighborhood zoned for livestock. Thus my childhood memories are filled with a variety of animals: cats, dogs, domestic rats, chickens, a rooster, a pony named Joe, multiple horses, various goats, and two kinds of pigs.

One of my first pets was a rooster named Elvis. I'm not sure why my parents thought that a rooster was a reasonable option for a pet, but it was definitely unique. I was fewer than seven years old at the time. The first few nights we had Elvis, I insisted he sleep inside our house; I was concerned that if he slept outside he would be cold and lonely. Thus my mother set up a pen for him in our enclosed patio which had an unused fireplace (again I question the appropriateness of a rooster as a pet for a suburban child). Oddly enough, Elvis the rooster chose to nest inside of the fireplace for a few days, before my parents banished him to the backyard. There he lived the rest of his life, sitting under the fig bush and perching in the avocado tree, waiting for me to visit and feed him.

Years later we had a formal, multitiered chicken coop that measured approximately ten by eight feet, with a large ground space and several nesting boxes. We kept a handful of chickens and never ate them, although it was my job to collect their eggs, which we did eat. I enjoyed my task of egg gathering. The chickens were an interesting group; some were quite chatty, while others were content to watch me from their perches.

With all these animals I would eventually come to experience death in a variety of ways: natural (my beloved rat Norman, whom I buried in a decorated shoe box) and tragic (our cat Grey, who was hit by a car). Perhaps the most disturbing were those animals who just disappeared. At one point we owned a pair of pygmy goats, a male and female. Eventually as the goats matured, the male, whom I had named Billy, became aggressive toward the female as well as humans. When they determined that this pet had worn out his welcome, my parents made a decision and one day Billy disappeared. I didn't ask questions but later overheard my parents' jokes that a man had come to take Billy away and he was probably turned into tacos. Why did Billy have to become tacos? He was our pet. Why had his behavior allowed us to turn him into something edible? If our other pets behaved badly, would they also be turned into food for humans?

When I became a vegetarian in my late twenties, I understood that we intentionally hide ourselves from the slaughter of animals. Yet when I read about this deliberate human tendency, it struck a nerve with me and I made a connection from my childhood.

One day my family brought home Pig. She was a tiny pink piglet with a black spot on her rump and was quite possibly the cutest pig ever. I had wanted to name her something pretty like Michelle or Sarah, but my mother coaxed me into naming her something more animal-appropriate; I thought it was strange my mother made such an issue of my name suggestions. I tried to think of something more appropriate, but nothing seemed to fit, and so Pig would be her name.

Pig lived in a nice pen with running water and lots of mud, and it was my responsibility to feed her. She quickly grew to be very large and not quite as cute, but still she was friendly and would greet me whenever I approached. She would trot the perimeter of her pen and grunt extra loudly, then for extra comedic flair she would stop in the center of the pen and turn in a complete circle before approaching me to be fed. Afterward she always seemed to want me to visit more, so I would scratch the length of her back, where her hair was coarse and caked in mud. This extra attention was met with squeals of gratitude and I quite enjoyed her playful responses.

Then one day, when I was about twelve years old, a man showed up to our house in a battered old truck. I noticed that the bed of the truck was lined with large pieces of plywood that were placed vertically to create a box. I can remember my mother's panic that I was present. I had been granted permission to go visit my friend's house but the man had arrived ahead of schedule. My mother quickly hurried me into the car and took me to my friend's house, and I quickly forgot about the man with the truck. When I returned home Pig, whom I had fed and befriended over the previous two years, had disappeared, and the freezer was now filled with packages that we would eat from for the next several months.

I was sad that Pig was gone, but I wasn't yet able to make the connection that I would now be eating my pet, whom I had cared for since she was a piglet. I had been hidden from this slaughter by my absence. My mother had been physically hidden from this slaughter by the wood lining in the truck. She had further chosen to hide herself from Pig's death by paying the man to complete the act while she was safe in our home. I wonder if she would have been able to eat Pig's flesh if she had witnessed Pig's carcass being butchered into portions that could be neatly packed into a freezer.

I know my mother intentionally hid me from the impending fate of Pig because she wanted to spare me pain. In my late twenties, all of my closest friends had become parents. I could see how much they loved their children and would do anything in their capacity to prevent their children from suffering. But what about the mothers who couldn't protect their young? Did mother animals feel pain when their young were forcibly removed? Could the mothers recognize the cries of their own offspring as they were marched into slaughter or forced into reproductive slavery? That was when the seeds of vegetarianism began to sprout in me.

Essentially I became a vegetarian for two reasons: my love for my dogs and an aversion to meat. When I read Carol Adams' account of her murdered pony and the hypocrisy of eating a hamburger, I understood what she meant. In our Western culture it is considered taboo to eat dogs and horses, yet in other cultures it is entirely permissible. Reciprocally, the same conflict occurs with eating cows or pigs, which we Westerners find permissible, while other cultures do not.

Presently I share my home with two Boston terriers, Skippy and Trixibelle. As any dog owner can attest, my dogs are excellent examples of reasoning and emotional beings who have developed a keen way of interacting with the world and its inhabitants. Although it could be considered simple and perhaps juvenile, at some point I realized that I would never eat my dogs, so how could I choose to eat other animals? What capacities did my dogs possess that justified them as inedible? The immediate response was that they were my companions and I had compassion for them. Was this the same reason why we didn't eat my pony or the other horses when I was a child? But why, then, was it acceptable to eat Pig? It wasn't. When I realized that my dogs had no other superiority over other animals, I knew I could no longer consume animals.

The second reason was a gradual change that took place within my own body. After a few years of being a vegetarian, I realized I had begun to associate meat with the body of another being, which had caused me to lose my taste for it. In *The Sexual Politics of Meat*, Adams mentions numerous instances in which women are not able to tolerate eating meat because they begin to restore the absent referent by thinking of meat as an animal carcass symbolic of their own oppression. Although I may not have been quite aware of that as a child, it's possible that my reaction to meat started as psychological rather than physiological. Even as a child I disliked eating beef, especially ground beef. I could rarely stomach dishes like meatloaf or ground beef tacos unless they were smothered in some sort of condiment. In my midtwenties I began to associate the look of a steak, with its sinewy strands and pink-brown hue, with the kind of human muscle chart that hangs in a doctor's office. I found that there was no condiment on earth that could transform a steak from a piece of human muscle tissue into something edible.

Although I'm a vegetarian, I'm not yet a vegan. I don't drink milk, yet I'm still an occasional consumer of certain dairy products, like cheese or ice cream (though I also eat the non-dairy versions of these products). I'm aware of the horrors of the dairy industry—the reproductive slavery that female animals are kept in—but when eating ice cream or cheese, it's easy to forget the invasive mechanized methods used to obtain the milk necessary for such products. How am I able to ignore this intentional hiding? What is the blockage that prohibits me from fully recognizing the oppression that I am participating in? Why have I not been able to fully commit to veganism? For each of these questions, I have multiple responses, yet no answer seems to be the right one or to be able to fully clear up my confusion.

I think back to the chicken coop from my childhood and wonder if that method of obtaining eggs was invasive and exploitative to the chickens. I feel guilty when I purchase eggs from the grocery store. Unlike the eggs that came from the chickens my family owned, the store-bought eggs were surely produced under conditions I would object to, yet I still buy and eat them. I wouldn't eat chicken flesh, because it requires the death of an animal—so am I still consuming eggs because they are something that can be produced by a live animal, albeit one that is commodified? Is the consumption of eggs that are obtained in a gentle manner justifiable?

Like the contradiction of compassion I see in my fellow shelter volunteers, I have contradictions of my own. I place such importance on the lives of animals, but not on the pain they must endure while intentionally kept alive. I will not eat their flesh, but I will still eat products of their bodies that have been forcibly harvested. I am stuck in some sort of self-imposed gray area. I theorize who I want to be—an ethical vegan—but I haven't been able to fully commit to it.

At home I prepare many vegan meals and I'm always excited to try a new recipe (I've amassed quite the collection of vegan cookbooks). I'll often go weeks without consuming a dairy product and then I slip. Whether it be a trusted dessert recipe from my past or a night out with friends in a restaurant, I inevitably bend and there is egg or cheese in what I'm eating. Something is inhibiting my commitment to veganism, but I'm not sure if it's any one thing. Perhaps it's a combination of things. Perhaps it's memories from my childhood—I enjoyed eating food like pizza and ice cream—or perhaps it's my fear of not being able to enjoy dining out in a restaurant with non-vegan friends. Or, it might be my fear of commitment—if I don't label myself as vegan, then surely I can't fail.

I see my own dilemma as a reflection of the contradictions that have surrounded me all my life. My family wouldn't eat the horses, but instead ate Pig. The shelter volunteers care for the dogs, but have no consciousness of the cows they eat. I won't eat animals, but I will use them. I'm not sure how to pinpoint the exact reason why my compassion is blocked, but I'm in constant negotiation with myself about how to move away from hypocrisy.

I do know this: I am trying to live in an ethical manner. I've taken many steps to become who I am today and will continue to work toward who I want to become. I am a feminist, I am a vegetarian. I am a not-yet vegan, but I am always in progress.

Opening Veins

KIM SOCHA

*C*ulture or biology? This too-easy binary often under-
lies conversations I have with the public during my animal advocacy
work. Are we biologically designed to eat animals or culturally motivated to do so? My honest answer is that it doesn't matter to me.
We live in an industrialized culture with ample alternatives to eating,
wearing, and otherwise using animals, so we shouldn't. And usually,
in activist contexts, it is unproductive and off-putting to get into an
esoteric critique of the binaries that plague us—human/animal (as
if humans aren't animals), man/woman (as if gender isn't a social
construct), good and evil (as if all of our actions could neatly fit into
one category or the other, ambiguity be damned!).

Carol Adams, through *The Sexual Politics of Meat* and her other
works, has helped me question the binaries and assumptions that
spring from Western culture's rationalist philosophical history. She
has set a foundation from which my nascent scholarship springs, and
I have carried her work's messages with me for the past twelve years
since I first read the book. However, my relationship with Adams'
work is ambiguous. I read her potent messages of interconnected
oppressions and female empowerment, but I didn't go vegan until

nine years later. In fact, I embarked on a self-destructive life journey, which I am still on, even as a vegan animal advocate and scholar, as well as an activist in other areas of social justice. Again, culture or biology? Am I driven to be self-destructive because of a woman-hating commodity culture, or is it biology, misfirings in the brain, that keep me questioning and silencing myself? *Most significantly, why has my self-destruction most palpably manifested through anorexia, drug addiction, and dependence on abusive men?* I wonder why I have a voice when defending nonhuman animals and the human animals I love, but when it comes to standing up for myself, I am often silent. And why, when not silent, do I feel I've done something wrong?

At a recent conference I read from my own book, *Women, Destruction, and the Avant-Garde: A Paradigm for Animal Liberation,* a book unabashedly and gratefully grounded in Adams' scholarship. I was angry (in the good way, against injustice) and empowered, and women approached me afterward with applause and appreciation. I felt like a motivating force because I told my truth in that book. And later, as I tried to fall asleep that night, I felt like a phony because I am still disempowered in so many ways, which is also my truth. That is the story I will tell here, a story that I won't hide behind erudition. But before I begin this story of destruction and renewal, I must offer a disclaimer: *I've gotten better, and I'm getting better.*

Writer Paul Gallico made the oft-quoted observation that "It is only when you open your veins and bleed onto the page a little that you establish contact with your reader." How fortunate I am that I get to do this metaphorically. Even as I write this, I think of all of the nonhuman animals who literally have their veins opened by the billions every year to satiate human desire for their flesh. That is what this story is: the tale of a self-destructive woman who finds her destruction metaphorically applicable to that of nonhuman animals, but privileged enough to find avenues out of that devastation; a woman who feels guilty for saying she has and does suffer when others suffer so much more. But to resist telling the story is to once again fall into the trap of self-silencing. Hence, the following attempt to "open my veins."

I'm also attempting to create an image of myself, a thirty-eight-year-old woman still seeking answers to the question "Who am I?" while grappling with the reality that she may never know. I look to the cover of *The Sexual Politics of Meat*, to that naked woman peering back with her red cowgirl hat, raven black hair, come-hither eyes, and crimson lips. She is both who I have wanted to be—a beautiful, desired woman—and what I despise being—a thing desired for her parts and then cast aside. She reminds me of Lynda Carter's Wonder Woman character that I so loved as a child—impossibly beautiful and strong, running around in as few articles of clothing as network television allowed in the 1970s. However, the woman on the cover does not have power. She is a product sectioned off into pieces, humbled and exposed. She is public property. Western culture has done this to her through its misogynistic media, it has done this to me, and it continues to do this to girls and women, at least figuratively, and to nonhumans, literally.

Then I flip in the book to the image of "Ursula Hamdress," the pinup pig who appears to pleasure herself with a subtle smile and a drink by her side. Ursula's image echoes the messages on the front cover. As an overweight teen, I had been called "pig," "cow," and "moose" by those from whom I sought acceptance. At the time, I thought those terms to be the lowest insults. To be animalized was to be reviled. For a woman, to be a "pig" is to be damned as an unwanted product, and although "fox" and "minx" are ostensibly compliments, they also damn women as objectified beings. In retrospect, I wish I had said to those who damned me, "Thank you! Pigs are intelligent, sensitive, and beautiful creatures." However, I was too far from the ideology of Adams' work during my teenage years to reply in such a manner. Instead of coming back at my tormentors with witty retorts, I developed anorexia.

Figure 1: The Starving Woman

I starved myself for about six years, from ages nineteen to twenty-five, resulting in two hospitalizations. While in the hospital, I met women like me: smart, funny, caring, and self-loathing enough to starve themselves in a land of plenty. We were also privileged enough to refuse food while others in the world starved due to lack of it. And we were fortunate enough to have parents or guardians who had the economic means to pay for our hospitalizations. Most of us in treatment were white, but there were women of color as well. In my experience, the starvers and bulimics were mainly white and the overeaters were predominantly women of color. However, and for whatever reasons, that disparity existed. The truth is that we were *all* using food to medicate ourselves for the simple yet complex reason that we did not like ourselves.

I made short-lived friendships while in the hospital. I think those bonds had a time limit because many of us were in competition with each other. At five-foot six inches tall, I weighed the least at eighty pounds, but I was living with women who were taller and thinner than me. I had trouble looking at them because they were so thin, and while their brittle hair and jutting bones repulsed me, I envied them too. They were "doing anorexia" better than me.

I was trying to be perfect by denying myself food, so I would no longer be labeled "cow" or "pig." I started losing weight and then I didn't stop. I wasn't consciously trying to mirror fashion models who starve themselves to be "marketable," but I was certainly bending under the cultural presumption that to be thin is to be of value. It was also my way of saying to the men who had teased me about my weight (and in my case, it was always men), "I'll show you."

A twisted "benefit" to my anorexia is that I also stopped feeling. Of course, I showed emotion. I was always crying, always reacting hyperactively to minor stressors as I graduated from college and made it through a master's program on as little food as possible. (Years later, when I started my Ph.D. program in 2006, seemingly far from the anorexia that once plagued me, this nagging voice in the back of my brain told me that the reason I had been so successful as a student was because I had been anorexic. How could I obtain a Ph.D. without starving myself? As it would turn out, one had nothing to do with the other.) My purposeful starvation shut me down as a woman. I stopped menstruating and developed osteoporosis at age twenty-three. I also had absolutely no sexual feelings of any kind. I considered these badges of honor, proof that I was at least doing anorexia somewhat right because everything else I did in my life seemed wrong or not good enough. Counting calories, exercising excessively, and trying to be an A student were all that mattered; they were the daily practices of a woman who didn't want to be a woman because she didn't think she could be visible in the "real world." She'd have no friends, she'd be incapable of loving or being loved by anyone other than her family, and she couldn't hold down a job and support herself financially. She would break if forced to sustain herself. The woman I imagined I would be wouldn't be able to do anything on her own.

I'm not sure what the official statistics are, but many of the anorexic women I met when I was in treatment also identified as vegetarian. In the mid- to late 1990s, I knew about veganism, but it wasn't nearly as popular as it is today, so there weren't many women claiming to be vegan at that time. In the course of their treatment, many of the vegetarian women I met started eating meat again. But not me. I prided myself for remaining so ethical even when I had pressure from the medical staff to eat meat. In retrospect, I don't blame them for assuming that vegetarianism was a way to limit fatty foods and food in general. However, it meant more to me than that, even back then. It was a matter of ethics.

Ethics, a system of proper action. I was starving myself into illness and I thought that I was being ethical. In reality, I was trying to be a force for those who are brutalized in our culture—namely, non-human animals—while sapping myself of any strength that might help me, and then them, to stop suffering. Yes, I had read *The Sexual Politics of Meat*, but I couldn't make the women-animals connection for myself. I couldn't see that *I* needed care, too.

Only now can I compare this passage in my life to the other females who are starved for profit—not supermodels, but hens who are denied proper sustenance anywhere from five to fourteen days in a distorted attempt to mirror nature, thereby forcing them to produce more eggs for financial gain. Even at my worst, I never went that long without eating. I ate every day, just not enough, and I would also work out for two hours every day, burning away the meager nourishment that I was taking in.

When I recovered from anorexia, after many stops and starts, I developed a coldness toward women with eating disorders. I claimed to have no sympathy for them. I eventually found the wherewithal to eat, so why couldn't they? How could they be so selfish and self-absorbed when people, especially children, were *actually* starving in areas of the globe ravaged by famine and war? Why should anyone care about purposeful starvers when there are families in the United States who cannot feed their children? I agreed with a George Carlin comedy bit about women with eating disorders: "Rich bitch, doesn't want to eat? Fuck 'er." I thought this lack of sympathy indicated that I had really beat anorexia, that I was free from self-imposed self-destruction, that maybe I never really had a problem to begin with.

But I did have a problem. And it wasn't just anorexia. And soon, it would simply shift shapes.

Figure 2: The *"Love"* and Drug-Addicted Woman

Culture or biology? Whichever of these (maybe both) made me anorexic made me "love" and drug addicted, too. For many people, these are two separate issues, but for me, as Roxy Music has claimed in a song, "Love is the drug for me." I put "love" in quotes because, of course, I never found love through any of my abusive relationships with men. Further, I *had* love in my life, from family and friends, but I still sought it from men who responded to me with emotional abuse, physical violence, obsession and, sometimes, simple disinterest. When approached by a stereotypical "nice guy," I would turn away with disinterest. I couldn't see spending time with a man who was kind to me, who thought I was okay, who didn't want to change me in some way. I was seeking someone who needed pleasing and/ or fixing. To be frank, I don't even know why men were so important to me. To this day, I question my sexuality. Over the years, I have labeled myself everything from heterosexual to bisexual to asexual to pansexual to whatever comes next. Labels aside—as I see it, they can be problematic and oppressive—the bottom line is that I sought and often still seek approval from men.

I came to my understanding of "love addiction" through a lengthy treatment for the seemingly more serious problem of drug addiction. Specifically, I became a cocaine and crack cocaine addict a couple years after recovering from anorexia. While in treatment, I was sent to Sex and Love Addicts Anonymous meetings because I had acted out sexually with a male patient. I laughed when they sent me to those meetings: I didn't even like sex, nor did I accept the notion of romantic love. Eventually, though, the meetings began to make sense, as did their connection to my cocaine obsession. There are chemicals in the brain that stimulate "love" addiction, just as there are chemicals in cocaine that simulate euphoria. Further, for me, drug addiction was tied to men, fueled by men, though I take full responsibility for my drug dependency. These addictions, unlike anorexia, nearly obliterated any ethical code I was still living by, especially in terms of my integrity and the integrity of nonhuman animals.

I once told a fellow animal advocate that after being vegetarian for ten years, I went back to eating meat for about three years. She winced when I said it; I could tell she was judging me. I'm sure she was wondering: How do you learn the truth about animal suffering and then unlearn it? I hadn't unlearned the truth; I just didn't care enough anymore. She, and other advocates I have met since becoming an activist, unwittingly remind me of how long it took me to internalize the truth rather than just know it. I hear about their extensive histories in the movement, replete with long-term veganism, feats of derring-do, animal rescues, et cetera. And then I think of the destructive addictions in which I was partaking while they were acting on conscience.

As bad as my anorexia was, drug addiction led me down a more sinister path. To this day, I include a return to meat eating as one of the many examples of how self-loathing, selfish, and pleasure-seeking I had become. Cocaine addiction made me care about nothing more than getting more cocaine. I did not care who I had to engage with to get it, where I had to go to get it, what I had to do to get it, who I had to hurt to get it, and how I would allow myself to be treated to get it. Thus, when I did eat, which would only happen every few days after coming down from a drug binge, I did not care who I was hurting to feed my starving body. In fact, with growing debt from credit card cash advances to buy drugs, fast food restaurants became cheap, easy places for me to purchase food. In sum, I began eating the literal fragments of tortured animal bodies because I was mentally tortured and figuratively fragmented.

I had a "partner in crime" during this period, a man on whom I had called the police at least twice because he was emotionally and physically abusive. He was a supposedly recovered heroin addict, so alcohol and cocaine seemed like child's play to him. I thought I loved him and I thought he loved me because he threatened suicide when I threatened to leave him, even holding a knife to his wrists once to prove he meant business. Again, how lucky we were that we could pretend to open veins when the animals we were eating had no say in the matter.

When we weren't high, and we did make attempts *not* to be high, we were hungry. And when we were hungry, we feasted on animal flesh. As he generally had no money, I would pay for our McDonald's runs and breakfasts at a nearby café where we would get cheese omelets and pork rolls (a Philadelphia thing). On special nights, we would go to a nearby pub, eat steak and drink wine (as if wine isn't a drug). However, despite the depths to which I sank during my addiction, I never truly felt like a meat eater. Rather, I felt like a vegetarian disguised as a meat eater because consuming animal flesh, even during my addiction, felt disgraceful somewhere in the back of my mind. This doesn't excuse my behavior, but I think there was a part of me that knew, or hoped, I would return to vegetarianism, though veganism still felt like an impossibility. The truths from *The Sexual Politics of Meat* were still there; I just didn't care enough to act on them. I didn't care about anything except feeding my addicted brain with cocaine and "love" from troubled men.

As I disregarded the bodily integrity of nonhumans, I disregarded my own as well. Not surprisingly, the illegal drug trade is run predominantly by men, and although I bizarrely prided myself on going into debt rather than bartering my body for drugs as I saw so many women do, if I'm to be honest, that is not the whole story. I stayed in abusive relationships to maintain a steady flow of cocaine, and, more than once, I used my sexuality to obtain it. I even had one man pull out a knife and force me to my knees, demanding that I pleasure him for crack. At the time, I shielded myself from the reality of the situation by claiming that he was my friend and that I owed him sex because he was supplying me with "free" drugs. Living like this, compassion had little to no place, not for myself, not for those who loved me, and not for the nonhuman animals I was eating.

Once again, as with anorexia, I had the luxury of recovery. And as I think of the treatment for which my parents paid more than $50,000, I feel shame even as I feel grateful. That money was offered to save me from an abusive relationship as much as it was to save me from cocaine addiction. Consequently, over the past five years, I have worked to help survivors of sexual abuse and domestic violence in rural locales and incarcerated youth in urban areas. So often, drugs and alcohol are a part of their victimization and incarceration. However, unlike me, they and their families do not have the financial means that enable them to be removed from the settings in which the violent drug trade flourishes. To this day, I am proud of overcoming cocaine addiction, but that pride is tainted by feeling like the little white girl whose mommy and daddy saved her from a corrupt culture, whereas many others cannot so easily find escape. The ambiguity always returns, as do the animals.

I have now been cocaine-free for about eight years. I've even found a way to use my experiences with addiction to help the non-humans I betrayed during my darkest days. At first, this connection surprised me. While I understood that anorexia can be tied back to the connections between speciesism and sexism, I didn't think that my hedonistic cocaine days would ever be anything other than a shadowy part of my history, another self-induced obstacle that I had overcome. Then, while volunteering at a Minneapolis-based animal liberation group, I was given the opportunity to take that lamentable history and do something positive with it.

Primates, rats, and mice were (and still are) being forcefully drug addicted in a research lab at the University of Minnesota, only a few miles from my home. One of the most horrific feelings I have experienced is coming down from a cocaine or crack high when there are no more drugs and no more money. To adequately put this feeling into words, I must paraphrase someone else, a strong woman of color who briefly acted as my sponsor during my recovery process. She put it like this: "You can't sleep. You can't be awake. You can't sit still. You can't move. Yet you try over and over to do all of these things. Your brain isn't working, but it is running so fast, urging you to find more coke. And if you can't, you are like a caged animal, a tiger pacing in a too-small cage." Once again, this is the extravagance of metaphor, but still a powerful statement about the destruction wrought by addiction.

The nonhuman animals at the University of Minnesota are *literally* pacing in cages, and they cannot sleep, cannot be awake, cannot sit still, and cannot move. I'm always loath to say that the aftermath of a drug binge is torture, but in the case of the primates, rats, and mice, that word is appropriate. As they suffer, someone is taking notes, someone is deciding when or if they get more cocaine, heroin, meth, nicotine, alcohol, and so on. Someone is watching them in their cages, assessing how long they will go without food as they "feen" for more drugs. Their parents cannot save them because they've been stolen from their parents. The government has not declared a war on drug-abused animals; in fact, the government is funding their addictions. And despite many local and national attempts to free them, the university, the law, and public disinterest makes it feel as if they will never be saved. Although addiction experts may disagree, these beings lack what I and other addicts had and have: a choice.

This research is ostensibly done for drug addicts like me; it's done to find behavioral and drug therapies to stop addiction. This research has been going on for over twenty-five years with little to nothing to show for it. I am profoundly disturbed that something I engaged in is connected with these experiments at the University of Minnesota, so I took part in a local campaign called "No Pain in My Name" in which former addicts and those affected by addiction attempt to have a say in how the research community goes about trying to "fix" us.

In this campaign, we tell our stories via brief video clips. In my interview, I explain the havoc that drug addiction wrought on my life, noting that I lost friends, the respect of my family, and that my career and life were put on hold. I then express dismay that nonhuman animals are being *forced* to feel the depression and isolation that I experienced as an addict. I also comment on an observation noted above: this research has been in progress for nearly a quarter century and it has yielded nothing to help those who suffer with addiction. (Though even if the research had been "successful," I personally do not think the ends would have justified the means.) My hope, and the hope of others who participate in the campaign, is to shame the university and paint the research for what it is—*inexcusable*, not a point of pride. As I explain in the video, I, and so many others I know, have recovered from addiction without benefit of whatever investigations and studies are taking place at the university. Though each of us shares different stories of drug and alcohol abuse and recovery, we all end with the final plea, "Don't cause pain in my name." There is enough pain that comes from choosing to continue one's addiction; we wish to end the pain that comes from forcing addiction onto others.

Figure 3: A Renewed, Imperfect Woman

At the 2012 Conference for Critical Animal Studies, I spoke about my book along with four other speakers—two men and two women—who also discussed their work. I was last to present, and as I watched and listened to the others, I noticed that when the women spoke, they stood behind the podium; when the men spoke, they either hung out casually by the side of the podium or moved around in front of the room, gesticulating dynamically. The women were heard, but also hiding themselves, albeit unconsciously. The men were heard, but felt no need to hide. What would I do? My gut reaction was, "I'm going to be like the men. I *won't* stand behind the podium!" Alas, I was driven behind the podium by cultural and/or biological forces;

I don't know which. I brought this up to the audience, and was later told by a few women that they, too, had noticed what I'd observed.

To this day, I'm at peace with having stood behind the podium, for as I argue in my book, our goal as women is not to be like men, just as we should not fight for animals to be like humans. Both of those battles devalue our authentic selves and the authentic selves of other species. Those battles subversively state that men set the paradigm for normalcy, as do humans. So, like the other women that evening, I hid my body, but also sounded my voice. In my talk, I explained that my book would not exist without Carol Adams' work as a theoretical foundation, nor could it exist without the love, compassion, and the emotions I feel when I think about the billions of nonhuman animals who suffer every day at human hands.

This is renewal. A woman who once starved and drugged herself into near oblivion achieved her goal of obtaining a Ph.D. She became vegan and an animal advocate. She also wrote a book through which she further attempted to establish connections among all cultural oppressions: that of women, nonhuman animals, those of the LGBTQIA community, the poor and the exploited. To use the ultimate cliché because it fits so well here: *I* found my voice.

But to this day, I don't always use it, even when I know that I should. And sometimes, I still silence myself in the hope of pleasing men. Nothing is clear, easy, or perfect, but I am getting better. I've realized that if I cannot advocate for myself in all contexts, I will never fully be able to advocate for other humans and nonhuman animals. The first step is acknowledging this and figuratively opening a vein so that my discomfiting truths can be known to the world; only then do I, and others who understand my story, have a better chance of sounding my truths without fear or pretense, as uncomfortable as those truths may be.

Dear Justice

MARLA ROSE

Dear Justice,

I'm a pretty fun mom, you have to admit. You know that I encourage running through sprinklers, a celebratory root beer every Friday after school, and sneaking up on Dad with a well-packed snowball. I'm not a stick-in-the-mud. Usually.

As my son, already the ripe old age of ten, you are also aware that I am not one who cedes easily when I believe in something. There are times when I must put my foot down. It may be hard to believe this but I don't refuse to allow you to eat pudding for dinner or spray the hose into the bedroom window simply because I enjoy the perks of being your personal Destroyer of Fun. You work that saucer-eyed, apple-cheeked angle, I'll give you that, but I have a job to do and part of it requires a certain resistance to your genetic advantages. There are actual benefits to my steadfastness, too, some of which you even reap: for example, you may not appreciate it now and you probably won't for years to come, but one day you'll be glad that I made you floss your teeth. Trust me on this. My stubbornness could also be interpreted as dedication: What would have happened if I'd decided to quit trying to give birth to you after two hours instead of going for the whole fifty-two hours? Well, you would have been born anyway, but I would have lost the opportunity to be your first positive role model. Yes, you were probably a little more preoccupied with that whole breathing and adapting to a completely new, amniotic fluid-free environment to appreciate it at the time, but I still like to think that your birth was my first life lesson to you.

If you believe in something with your whole heart, *never* give up. I believe in veganism and feminism with my whole heart and I always have, even before I was a vegan feminist myself. It just took me a while to realize it and then fuse thought with action; but once I did, there was no turning back.

Where did these two strands originate and how did they come to twist around each other and merge together? I'd say that it's because the third strand, my lifelong passion for justice, provided the piece that braided it together, entwining them to each other, to itself, and to me. Was there ever a doubt that one day I would give my child such a formidable name as yours?

It's impossible to know when the kernel for my burgeoning feminist consciousness was first planted but it may have been when I was four and a boy named Peter from down the street—he was really awful—told me that girls were inferior to boys, causing me to ball up my little hands and scream, "We are not!" in his stupid ear. Or maybe the root found its source when I was a little older, when some cigar-chomping great uncle or another told me that I shouldn't try too hard to win at board games because competitive girls were "unattractive." It could have also been the stories I glimpsed in the newspaper and on television about the Equal Rights Amendment and the resistance to it that set things into motion. (What was so controversial about equal rights, for goodness sake? What what what?) Before these events and a million others chipped away at my naïveté, though, I was blissfully unaware that there was ever even a reason to be a feminist.

I would say that I was born with feminist sensibilities, but to me this presumes that as a young child I thought girls were in any way not equal to boys, which I certainly did not. In many ways, I was fortunate to grow up in the 1970s, an era during which my friends and I would have been deeply offended if anyone had dared to imply that we were princesses, an insult of the highest order. Across the province of Romona Road and the two blocks on either side, my friends and I climbed trees, thwarted bullies, skinned our knees, drafted peace treaties, drew elaborate treasure maps, put on plays, dodged whoever was tagging, spied on suspicious characters, were entrusted to care for toddlers, created museum-quality sidewalk drawings, and rescued stray animals. Poofy satin dresses, scepters, and tiaras would have been completely impractical attire, not to mention annoying and insulting.

If the Instamatic photos I have are a good window into that era, it was a much more gender-neutral time and the default gender was distinctly unisex: we wore orange-and-green plaid jumpsuits and wouldn't have bothered with anything that limited our ability to stop, drop, and roll like firefighters in training. The world was open to us being who we were, girls and boys alike—at least that was what Marlo Thomas told us. My dirt-dusted friends and I didn't know that we were feminists because we were busy doing the important work of just being us. We were guided by our own inner compasses and our passions, blissfully ignorant of the need for feminism.

My ignorance didn't last long. You may not know how crushing it feels to learn that you need a social justice movement to support your right to be fully you. When you're someone who negotiates tough neighborhood disputes and drafts maps with sensitive territories before lunch, it does not seem at all fair for a good reason. It's not.

As I got older and moved farther from the more level playing field of early childhood, the inequality of the world increasingly seeped into my awareness. The idea that we weren't all born with the same opportunities because of arbitrary factors outside of our control caused me to be deeply disappointed in adults. Weren't they the ones in the driver's seat? If they were in charge of the world, why couldn't they outlaw discrimination? At the very least, why couldn't they be better examples?

To a child, so much revolves around the concept and maintenance of fairness; this is as true today as it was when I was when I was your age. Anyone who tried to swindle at a game, steal extra candy or sneak unfair advantages for him- or herself was considered to be a cheater, which was pretty much the worst thing anyone could be—at least, that was the prevailing sentiment on Romona Road. You could be an inferior bike rider, you could have a nervous bladder, you could be a whiner who was worthless at climbing trees, but being a cheater was the lowest rung on the ladder of personal defects. That was the one thing that could irreversibly taint one's reputation. Cheating said something about one's character and what it said wasn't pretty. Keeping others from their natural rights was stealing from them and with so much inequality in the world, it was clear that we were ruled by a federation of overgrown cheaters.

Justice, you came into this world full of guileless innocence and your innate sense of fairness and equality remains intact. I am proud to say that you have no prejudices outside of being vaguely suspicious of everyone who works in your dentist's office. Knowing this, I can say that one day the inequities of the world will make you just so disappointed and that disappointment will turn into anger. I'm truly sorry for that but it's probably necessary and I have no doubt that you can work through it to something that's productive for you.

The way the world is, the unfairness of it, isn't my fault, but now that I am an adult, I'm sort of implicated too, right? At ten, you know how brutally some beings are treated simply for not having been born human. You feel with your kind, expansive heart how unfair this is. You are as awestruck by an ant carrying a crumb as you are a strange bird swooping through the sky. You understand their right to autonomy because you are also a truly free spirit.

When I became a vegetarian at age fifteen, just five years older than you are now, it was quite simply because it felt like the right thing to do. The spark was lit when I had a biology class that included dissection my sophomore year; it changed the whole trajectory of my life. As a result of that unit, I could no longer deceive myself about what I ate: the fetal pig, suspended in formaldehyde, entombed before birth in a jar, became burnished in my mind's eye forever. I can still smell the sickening formaldehyde of that classroom. It smelled like something worse than death: it smelled like an atrocity. From the first day I saw those pigs, whether it was my grandmother's once-beloved brisket or a turkey sandwich at the school cafeteria, I could no longer detach from what was on my plate. This "food" had been an animal and it was not too different from the fetal pig in biology class. It was violence and cruelty on a plate and it was completely unnecessary. That biology class altered something in me—a resonance, a consciousness—that never quite shifted back. From that point on, I saw the world with a new lens. That fetal pig had become the ultimate object—born dead, born to be eviscerated and discarded—and I rejected that objectification with my whole being.

In college, my activism flourished. At a student organization fair early my first year, I signed up for every progressive group

I could find, including the Creative Anachronists, having mistakenly read their sign-up sheet as one for Creative Anarchists. (That first meeting was confusing for me, what with all the talk about the finer points of jousting etiquette and members who bowed as they referred to me as "m'lady." I was unsure about the meaning of anarchy for quite some time following this.) I circulated petitions; slept overnight in a mocked-up shantytown on campus; took an interminably long, cramped bus ride from the Kansas cornfields to Washington, D.C.; protested something or another and headed immediately back to the prairie; argued with Young Republicans in my dorm (buzzing on chocolate-covered espresso beans); came home for winter break and castigated my parents for being materialistic and parochial. While I was walking to class, I was thinking about progressive politics. While I was in line at the cafeteria, I was thinking about social justice movements. While I wasn't shaving, I was thinking about how the personal is political. I lived, breathed, and ate Important Ideas. In short, I was a delight.

One day, I was looking through the feminist theory section of our student union bookstore and I happened upon *The Sexual Politics of Meat*. Reading this book, this brave, lacerating, nakedly truth-telling opus, created another fundamental shift within me that wouldn't allow me to revert back to my previous state. Just as seeing those dead fetal pigs in the jars, floating until we were instructed to start cutting them apart, caused me to see the world in a whole new light and thus informed my path; so too did reading Carol Adams' book. Although I had already been a feminist and a vegetarian, I realized while reading this book how deeply damaging objectification is to those who are turned into so-called others and to society as a whole. It is not funny, cheeky, and innocent fun. Objectification is the process and pathway through which one is devalued, fragmented, stripped of individuality and, ultimately, destroyed.

The Sexual Politics of Meat taught me never to silence the voice that speaks truthfully about what I see and what is concealed. The year that I read Carol Adams' book, I graduated with a degree in fine arts. In the years that followed, I started following my true passion and became a writer, I think in no small part because Adams' book had such an unflinching vision woven through it that in reading it, I also found freedom to see my own path. As with becoming vegan, once you see, you cannot "unsee." You can turn it off. You can dial it down. You can pretend that you no longer see. Make no mistake, though: your perspective has been fundamentally altered. The light that the book shone on the deeply obfuscated and the horrifyingly ordinary, the plainly stupefying and the shrewdly cunning, was nothing to be afraid of, I learned. We also shouldn't be afraid of what was hidden. We just had to truly look, Adams showed us through her example, and we had to be honest about what we saw. *The Sexual Politics of Meat* taught me that there were worse things than speaking the truth despite the pressure to ignore it.

So, Justice, here's where you come into things. Before you were born, your father and I had your name picked out but we knew that it was a very powerful name, one that would easily overwhelm a newborn who couldn't meet the challenge. We had some alternate names in the lineup just in case and we were more than willing not to decide on your name until we had a good sense of you. After that 52-hour labor, though, the one in which you struggled so valiantly to be born, you came out kicking and screaming and giving everyone in that room a piece of your mind. We had no doubt that that moment you were most definitely a Justice. Since the day you were born, you have been speaking your truth, swimming against the current, if that feels right to you, creating the sort of world you want to live in and lovingly, steadfastly holding on to your core values of fairness and compassion.

You were born into a mess and I'm sorry that I haven't been able to clean it up more. Every time we see an image of a segmented woman or a segmented chicken, I feel like apologizing to you, embarrassed of this world you were born into, the screwed-up values here. Ever since you were born, my instinct has been to cover your eyes and your ears and let you keep believing that the world is a better, more just place. I know that I can't shelter you forever. You were born into the same world that I was born into, the one that I thought I could change through sheer force of will. I haven't given up on that, you know. I don't think that you will, either.

At the very least, I know that the legacy of one vegan feminist will live on and your vision will help to morph your convictions into something exquisite, unique, and necessary to this world. I love watching you continue to unfold, my boy. The gifts that you will bring into the world already have me sitting on the edge of my seat.

So, Justice, never give up. You may not see the changes you want to see immediately—you may not ever—but you will do your very best and that is no small thing.

Love always,

Mom

Chicken

The Feminist-Vegan's Dilemma

COLLEEN MARTELL

Although I am a newly minted Ph.D. in English and women's studies who teaches and uses *The Sexual Politics of Meat* in my research, I must confess that I often can only read the book one section at a time because of its potential to anger, sadden, and hurt. I'm reminded of the dominance of the meat-eating and patriarchal cultures and how they've affected my life. I'm reminded that my passion for vegetarianism has been laughed at, rejected, denied. It also brings to the surface my interconnected feelings of responsibility and failure: my responsibility to practice and teach compassion for all living beings, and my failure to inspire those around me to make a change.

To give an example of a recent failure, my partner and I were out at a diner-like restaurant (read "not vegan-friendly") with his parents and an old friend of his from college after a Friday night slo-pitch softball game. Of course my order was conspicuous because of my many questions to the server: "Is it possible to get a gyro without meat? Does your sauce contain dairy? Is there any other dairy in the wrap? Do you have any dressings that do not contain meat, dairy, or eggs?" Yes, yes, yes, and no. "Ok, thanks. I'll have a gyro, no meat, no sauce, no cheese." The topic at our table then turned to veganism. My partner's friend asked me why I am vegan and if it is for health reasons. I answered that, yes, it is for health reasons and then disappeared into my dry shredded lettuce and tomato on a pita so as not to have to discuss this anymore. My partner—not a vegetarian— then offered that my veganism was for other reasons as well, including environmental, moral, and ethical reasons. Yes, I agreed, that's true, too. At some point later it hit me: I was no longer the outspoken animal rights activist that I had been for most of my childhood and adolescence. Somewhere along the way, education and raising awareness about vegetarianism became less important than making omnivores feel comfortable with their meat-eating so that I could be left alone to eat in peace, free from criticism and prejudice. What had happened to me?

When I read *The Sexual Politics of Meat* for the first time as a twenty-year-old vegetarian and burgeoning feminist, it felt like coming home. But it is not always easy to return home. *The Sexual Politics of Meat* also brought me face-to-face with the effects of a childhood and adolescence full of intrusive questioning and even abusive behavior from my meat-eating peers. In addition to providing me with a language with which to name my experiences, the book also gave me a heritage of feminist-vegetarian foremothers (and fathers) and a fellow feminist-vegan searcher, writer, and activist in Adams herself. This resonated because, of course, I already had a feminist-vegetarian foremother in my own mother.

My mother and I became interested in vegetarianism through her younger brother. He began talking to her—while I listened intently—about the vegetarian lifestyle over weekly family dinners at my grandparents' house. This was around 1986, when I was seven years old. "Do you know where the chicken on your plate comes from?" he'd ask. "Have you ever heard of a factory farm?" She hadn't. A recent convert to Buddhism, my uncle educated himself about animal cruelty as part of practicing *ahimsa*, or nonviolence. He recommended books and films, told her about fur trapping and factory farm practices. He informed her about animal testing for cosmetics and other products. She decided to try a vegetarian diet for three months, but after reading Peter Singer's *Animal Liberation* and John Robbins' *Diet for A New America*, she knew she would never go back to eating meat. For my mother a decisive moment was reading an article about a butcher in the Sunday paper. Acknowledging that she herself could not slaughter an animal, she realized that she couldn't continue to ask another person to kill living beings on her behalf. To my young mind the decision was simple: once the connection was made between the beautiful living beings I loved as pets or saw on our trips to local farms and the dead "food" on my plate, I could no longer participate in a practice that now seemed so cruel.

I was fortunate to have a parent with whom to make this journey. I never felt pressured to change my diet; my mother and I made the decision together and supported each other however we could. My mother recalls one uncomfortable dinner where she hid a serving of meat she had been craving behind her mashed potatoes so I wouldn't see it! In this and other ways we held each other accountable as we made the transition. My consciousness changed as well as my diet. I no longer saw a mouth-watering steak on television commercials, but instead saw the suffering animal that "steak" once was. A hot dog looked to me like a screaming pig on a bun. As other adults oohed and aahed over the sight of a toddler eating an adult-sized hot dog or hamburger, we viewed it as a child's cruel indoctrination into the culture of animal consumption. Within two months of deciding to go vegetarian as a seven-year-old, I knew I had made a lifetime commitment. I had found a new home.

In many ways I had an idyllic vegetarian childhood. I grew up in the 1980s in Bethlehem, a small working-class city in eastern Pennsylvania best known for its steel production during and after World War Two. Our home was full of vegetarian pamphlets, books and, of course, great food. Though my father never gave up meat, he supported my mother's transition to vegetarianism as well as her desire to raise me and my siblings as vegetarians. I already had a younger sister and brother who also went vegetarian when my mother and I did. My mother had two pregnancies after that, so there were six vegetarians in my house: my mom and five kids. The seven-member Phoenix family, including River and Joaquin Phoenix, was my vegetarian role model. A 1987 guide book for vegetarian parents by Michael Klaper entitled *Pregnancy, Children, and the Vegan Diet*, which I read many times, featured their stories and made my big vegetarian family feel normal—even cool. Here was a community to which I belonged. My family ordered a lot of our food from catalogs because it wasn't easy to find natural and vegetarian foods in our local grocery stores. My grandfather, retired and a phenomenal cook, happily added a cornucopia of delicious vegetarian food to our Saturday evening family dinners.

Vegetarianism wasn't just about food to us, though; it was a lifestyle. My family worked hard to recycle much of what we used long before our city had any sort of pick-up system. We also stopped using laundry and dish detergents, household cleaners, soaps, and other toiletries that contained animal products, and volunteered at animal shelters. We talked about and practiced compassion in our daily lives in the way we treated one another and other living beings. A big family in a congested row home, we were encouraged by my mother to respect one another and value one another's space. We were also encouraged to be aware of others' experiences, not only to see the world through our own eyes. Whether it was spiders or our rescued companion animals, trees and plants outside, or our siblings in the house, we practiced respect, kindness, and forgiveness. Already an avid reader, I voraciously read vegetarian children's newsletters and cookbooks, even publishing an acrostic poem in a zine called "Otterwise." Looking back, my play on the zine's title reads like my childhood activist manifesto:

> **O**ther
> **T**hings
> **T**hat live on
> **E**arth have
> **R**ights too.

We spoke up about vegetarian ideology, proudly wearing shirts like, "WHY EAT SOMETHING DEAD TO STAY ALIVE?" and attaching a bumper sticker to our huge, rundown Dodge van that read, "VEGETARIANS ARE SPROUTING UP ALL OVER." We were such a big family, and since I was also surrounded by a vegetarian aunt and uncle and cousins, it seemed to me that vegetarians were, indeed, sprouting up all over.

From the vantage point of seven years of age, I did not see how abnormal my family was. To me, my vegetarian home was warm and compassionate, but to many of my peers it seemed more like an alien planet. I was moved by what I saw, read, and discussed with my mother. I believed that if others could see what I saw, they too would never eat dead animals again. Looking back now, I can see that I was poorly prepared for being a vegetarian outside of my home and in a world where most people ate meat. It was lonely growing up vegetarian in a conservative Catholic school environment. More than lonely: I was an easy target by speaking so openly and so passionately about animal rights.

With optimism I took on the responsibility of informing my larger community about animal abuses. Besides bringing in vegan birthday treats (Tofu Chocolate Chip Cookie Bars were my favorite) and abstaining from meat at school events (it became a family specialty to eat ketchup on a bun sans hamburger) I used every opportunity of a report or project to educate my fellow students about the horrors of animal cruelty. For example, I once made a poster that displayed the graphic suffering of monkeys and rabbits subjected to testing for hair spray and cosmetics. My poster was a collage made from animal rights pamphlets; the center image displayed a side view of a rabbit whose skin and fur were burned off due to repeated cosmetics testing, framed with other photos of abused animals, along with facts and statistics. But my teacher dismissed it by saying that human safety was more important than that of animals. In general, my attempts to open my classmates' eyes to animal cruelty were almost entirely ignored, misunderstood, or silenced by all of my teachers.

One year my mother offered to speak to my fifth-grade class on the topic of vegetarianism. She had been an elementary school teacher before she stayed home to take care of me and my siblings and, although she's since gone back to graduate school and changed careers—a decision central to my own feminist awakening and to my graduate work—she's always had a gift for teaching. Her presentation was lively, moving, and compelling. We did a vegetable-themed word puzzle and vegetarian-food brain teasers, a worksheet on identifying favorite common vegetarian foods (macaroni and cheese! spaghetti!) and some not-so-common foods (tempeh, carob, and papaya), discussed ways of being young activists (start a poster campaign, ask your family to plan and cook one vegetarian meal a week), and a game on matching famous vegetarians such as Benjamin Franklin, Albert Einstein, Mister Rogers, and Cyndi Lauper with their accomplishments.

We watched and discussed segments of a 1986 film by Tom Regan called *We Are All Noah*, which examines the value of animals in faith traditions. The film's central question is, "How should an informed compassionate religious ethic respond to animal cruelty?" We first watched a scene in which Regan asks school-age children to describe their image of a farm, which was mostly characterized by roaming animals and green grass, contrasted by footage and descriptions of factory farming. We then watched a segment that showed Jewish and Christian ceremonies for blessing animals. During these scenes religious leaders respond to the film's guiding question, arguing that no matter what the faith tradition, we are asked to make gentle our bruised world, to be compassionate toward all.

My mom did not force any beliefs onto my classmates. She simply encouraged them to ask questions and tried to help make vegetarianism normal. "This is how some people feel and think about animals," she told us. "Maybe having dominion over animals and the earth doesn't mean we can do with them whatever we want," she proposed, "but means we should be compassionate stewards for their lives." Sensitive to the fact that we were minors, my mother repeated that we all needed to follow our parents' advice, and that this was just another way of thinking about our relationships with animals. I was excited to see my classmates talking about the same issues me and my siblings talked about. Lunch that day was not awkward or uncomfortable, but a thrilling discussion of the issues concerning the bologna and turkey sandwiches in my friends' lunch bags: Where did that food come from? What other kinds of sandwiches might they eat? My friends now saw what I saw, what later in life I would read Adams describe in *The Sexual Politics of Meat* as animals made absent through language, definition, and metaphor in the way we name, understand, and talk about them as food.

That night, many of my classmates refused to eat the meat on their plates at dinner. Their parents were outraged. Our principal, a supportive and kind nun, received numerous angry phone calls from parents condemning my mother's presentation. In response, my teacher lectured us first thing that next morning. "It is perfectly okay to eat meat and animal products. There is nothing wrong with eating animals," he said. My heart sank. Other students raised objections, recalling what they'd seen on the factory farm, but our teacher firmly continued, "Eating meat is healthy and necessary." I protested that my family was healthy and didn't eat meat, but he wasn't swayed. "Colleen's family is different," he insisted. "Colleen's mother is wrong." My protests were dismissed in front of the class, and I was also taken out into the hall. "You must stop speaking to other students about vegetarianism," he admonished me. End of discussion.

After that incident, my ability to feel at home outside of my family became increasingly complicated: I belonged to a community of my peers but I suppressed much of my identity. My eighth-grade science teacher, the mother of one of my classmates, told our class that I was going to die before everyone else my age because the vegetarian diet is unhealthy. She said my bones would shrivel and break, my heart would fail, my hair would fall out. I wasn't getting enough protein; I was weak and wouldn't live very long. Because she was a science teacher, everyone believed her. In high school I failed a unit on dissection because I refused to dissect a frog and baby pig.

In my junior and senior years other students would regularly throw meat from their sandwiches at me and on my food. This wasn't part of a larger experience of harassment; it was specifically about freaking out the vegetarian. It was also about gender: the particular way I was harassed had something to do with boys enjoying making a girl squirm. When I think about these experiences I'm proud that I stayed committed to vegetarianism, but I'm also sad that I was so alone in these beliefs that I ended up not talking about them at all.

Over the course of twenty years I moved from sharing my passion for animal rights with my classmates to sharing it only with my close friends, until I found myself at age twenty-seven evading questions over dinner at a diner with my non-vegetarian partner. College turned out to be a more supportive place for vegetarians, but I was still the only one I knew outside of my family. I belonged to a small community of vegetarians in college when my roommate of four years and my girlfriend of five years both went vegetarian, but this was short-lived. Not long after graduation my roommate went back to eating meat and my girlfriend did as well after we broke up. And although my strict vegetarianism gradually became veganism in my late twenties, my three youngest siblings began eating meat sometime in high school, leaving only my mother, myself, and one sister as vegetarians. Vegetarianism slowly became more of a personal decision than a social issue in my life.

It wasn't until graduate school that I met more vegetarians. This is also the place where I encountered the strongest and most vocal enclave of feminists, though the two only rarely overlap. At last I felt a sense of belonging to a community. A group of eight to ten of us have vegan/vegetarian potlucks once a month, volunteer at animal sanctuaries, and share recipes, tips (such as, always travel with hummus!), and horror stories of life as vegetarians (the guilt and anxiety of refusing a special dish someone made you because they unknow-ingly thought vegans eat butter). Much to my and my mother's shock, vegetarian and vegan food has become much more mainstream than it was when my eighth-grade science teacher informed our class that this lifestyle is (deathly) unhealthy. Veganism is practically trendy. As a result, my community has physically widened, my definition of community has expanded, and I feel more at home.

However, I'm still left with a number of questions: How can I maintain passion and fervor for a minority view in such a way that every meal doesn't become a war zone? Is my goal as a committed feminist-vegan to convince all those around me to subscribe to my beliefs? If not, then what are the goals? Is it enough to do as count-less bloggers and cookbook authors suggest and simply continue serving meat eaters delicious vegan food in the hope that they'll eat less meat? Where's the balance between my zealous childhood veg-etarianism and my introverted adult veganism? How do I reconcile my hope for a world without the abusive and exploitative consump-tion of the flesh and secretions of animals and my desire to simply eat in peace? This question easily expands: How do I reconcile my hope for a world without abuse or exploitation of any beings with my longing for community in the larger culture?

It all boils down, finally, to one question: How do I bring theory into practice without alienating those around me and getting myself hurt?

An important piece is acknowledging that veganism and femi-nism are far from home for many people. Beef, chicken, cow's milk, eggs: these things are home to a large portion of the population. They represent family gatherings, traditions, memories, recipes passed down for generations. I take great pleasure in veganizing my grandfather's Pennsylvania Dutch filling recipe—a traditional holiday dish made from mashed potatoes, bread, onions, celery, and sea-soning that's easily made vegan by substituting vegan versions of milk, butter, and broth. For many others substitutions or omissions for long-standing traditions might threaten the foundation of who they are.

Being a feminist is perhaps not quite as difficult, at least in my case. I officially identified as a feminist years after I'd identified as a vegetarian, but the connection between them seemed obvious to me. I was learning in every women's studies course that gender was interrelated with class, race, sexuality, et cetera, and so it made sense to a longtime animal rights supporter that justice, oppression, and objectification applied to nonhuman beings as well. But animal rights aren't sanctioned by academia the way gender studies is. I have my "Introduction to Gender Studies" students write about and discuss their perceptions of feminism on the first day of class. Inevitably the responses go something like this: "Feminists are radical bra-burn-ing, man-hating women who don't shave their legs and march in the streets yelling about inequality." They are shocked, then, to discover that by believing that women should have the right to equal pay for equal work, should have reproductive rights, and should not be treated as objects, they themselves are feminists. Later in the semes-ter when my students read excerpts from *The Sexual Politics of Meat*, they understand Adams' argument about gender, but laugh at her argument about consuming the flesh and secretions of animals. Just like their initial impressions of feminism, they cringe at what they perceive as a radical argument. No one wants to be too radical, too far from home.

In my efforts to be a feminist-vegan activist I seem to make the same mistakes over and over again. When the things that I'm fight-ing for are both so personal and political—whether it's food on my plate or control over my body—it is easy to take others' defensiveness too personally, set high expectations, and let emotion rule the discussion. When dealing with a sense of responsibility—to siblings, friends, students, animals, the environment, yourself—it's easy to get burned out, to feel alienated, to be pulled in overwhelming directions.

What, then, are my goals as a feminist-vegan activist? Where is home for me now? It doesn't make sense to me to go back to my naïve childhood activism, when I truly believed if everyone saw what I saw, they'd simply never eat animals again. The self-deprecating vegan doesn't feel right either. If my diet makes omnivores feel defensive, then perhaps that's something worth analyzing rather than avoiding. Yet I have to accept that vegetarianism is a big step for many people, that not everyone will feel like I do, and that nobody likes being told what to do or how to act. While I've convinced friends, family, and even strangers that vegan food can be delicious, this hasn't stopped them from consuming animals. Even my incredibly supportive partner of six years, who stuck up for me over dinner at the diner and eats a strict vegetarian—almost vegan—diet in our home, still eats meat sometimes. At times I feel saddened by his animal consumption, but what's most important is that I recognize that he is trying to meet me halfway.

I'm surprised to realize that I take a different stance when it comes to teaching gender studies. I know I'm not convincing every student in my classes to support feminism, but it's enough for me that I've taught them to ask good questions about the world around them and to be critical of oversimplified answers. Maybe that's the best I can do with animal rights as well. Over twenty years ago Regan concluded his film *We Are All Noah* by stating that asking the right questions is the first step at arriving at the right answers. Maybe

I don't need to choose between the ardent activism of my youth or remain in a repressed self-effacing state of veganism. Accepting this doesn't mean I won't still feel frustration, hurt, or sadness, but it may mean that I'm better at listening, more easily heard by others, and ultimately more compassionate. Greater acceptance of the challenges of feminist-vegan activism might also mean that the next time I'm at a roadside diner and am asked about my veganism, I am able to say, without defensiveness or fear, "Yes, I am vegan for health reasons, and for me health implies more than simply my own physical health. I believe veganism is one of the most effective ways of creating greater physical, emotional, and spiritual health and well-being for myself, other humans, animals, and our planet." This self-confidence and honesty may open up opportunity for dialogue and even change. And a world with more thoughtful and compassionate reflection is, after all, my intention.

This past Christmas my traditional vegetarian-themed gift from my mom was a T-shirt that reads, "I'm Vegan and I Love You." I think my biggest mistake has been to let hurt and sadness close me off from others to the point that this message of love seemed only meant for other feminist-vegans. Though I'm still a work in progress, I'm moving toward being more at home in a feminist-vegan mind-set of love and compassion even—and especially—for those with whom I disagree. Because although my history as a vegetarian is marked by pain, in looking back I can see that from the very beginning it's also characterized by love and kindness for all beings.

Cripping the Sexual Politics of Meat

SUNAURA TAYLOR

I was a graduate student receiving my MFA at UC-Berkeley when I was first introduced to Carol Adams' book *The Sexual Politics of Meat.* I had no thought that I would learn something about disability from the book; I bought it as most people do, because of my interest in animal rights.

A lot was happening for me at that time, not least of which was the endless hours of studio work I did every week painting a giant ten-foot-by-eight-foot canvas of hens on a chicken truck en route to a slaughterhouse. I was thinking about these birds every day, staring at the photographs I was working from, wondering about what had happened to them when they had arrived at the slaughterhouse. This work spilled over into my drawings, into other paintings, into what I was reading and thinking about. I had no idea what I was getting myself into when I had initially decided to paint that painting. I soon became known as the "chicken lady" within the Berkeley Art Department.

If there is one thing that has led me to where I am now in my thinking about animals and about disability, it is a memory I have growing up in Georgia. Summers in Georgia are sweltering, humid, sticky, and uncomfortable. I have vivid memories of driving along the highways in our family vehicles that seemed always to lack air-conditioning—being too hot to move, and drinking massive amounts of water and soda from Big Gulp cups we'd get from the air-conditioned strip malls where we'd run our errands. It was a common experience to look out our car windows and see rows and rows of chickens on massive fast-moving trucks. These chickens were alive, often packed so tightly beside one another that the truck itself seemed to have feathers. The chickens were clearly dying, slowly being cooked as they zoomed down the road. They were scraggly, terrible-looking birds, sometimes literally falling through the wire cages that held them in.

These trucks were horrible to my siblings and me. They were profound moments of cruelty whirring by constantly and no one seemed to notice. The three of us would hold our breath every time we saw one until it passed us. Originally this started because the smell was so horrendous—with our windows down, we could smell the dying birds and chicken feces cooking in the heat before we'd even notice the truck was beside us—but eventually holding our breath became more symbolic—to not breathe was a way of recognizing that something deeply wrong was happening right beside us.

After our initial realization as young kids that meat was *animals*, my brother Alex, sister Astra, and I went through a few years of on-and-off animal rights activism. We read books like *Kids Can Save the Animals: 101 Easy Things to Do* and we set up information tables at our local Earth Day festivals. When I was about eleven my siblings (by this time there were four of us—I had another sister, Tara) and our friends went through a phase of making angry calls to fur coat manufacturers. Yet despite our young radicalism, animal issues existed in the background of my thoughts for the most part. Being a vegetarian and caring about animals had been a part of my identity for so long—I became vegetarian by choice when I was about six years old— that as I grew older it became something that I lived out of habit, but never really thought about. I would hold my breath as the chicken trucks went by, but I never thought to consider those birds beyond simply feeling that it was wrong to eat them.

My sisters and brother, however, each went through phases as they became adolescents of researching animal issues, thinking about them philosophically, and forming more nuanced and informed opinions of the choices they were making. Even my younger sister Tara, who had been born after my family had become vegetarian, went through a period of considering critically this philosophy into which she had been born. One after the other my siblings each did the research and thought about the issues seriously—each eventually coming to the conclusion that they would become vegan.

I didn't go in this direction, partly because I never felt so inclined to research everything as my siblings had, and perhaps because I was too consumed by trying to figure out how to survive as a disabled kid. Veganism just didn't make sense—it seemed like an extreme dietary restriction that had little impact on the world. It also just seemed hard for me, as someone who used a wheelchair and largely relied on other people to cook for me or on easy-to-prepare microwavable dinners. But mostly it seemed hard because I loved certain foods— I was a mac 'n' cheese kid. I had always loved cheesy omelets and creamy things of all kinds and I couldn't really grasp in a visceral way why these things could be wrong.

I blame my love of macaroni for my general lack of desire to actually research this thing that I supposedly held so dear. I was a passionate vegetarian, but looking back I don't think I really knew why I was so passionate. My instinctual feeling was that chicken trucks were cruel, but I was unaware of the depth and pervasiveness of the systems and ideologies from which that cruelty had grown.

Like so many things in life, I eventually found myself confronting these topics when I least expected it and in an unlikely area of my life. In 2006 I applied to UC-Berkeley. I had been painting seriously for many years and wanted to go to graduate school for an MFA. Before I left Georgia for California I decided I wanted to paint one of these chicken trucks that I had so often seen during my life.

I had learned a few months prior that I unknowingly lived a few blocks away from a chicken "processing" plant (the final destination of these trucks). As so often happens, this massive industry was somehow invisible to most moderately well-off people in our city, tucked away on strange out-of-the-way roads, where the pollution, smell, and terribly paid, largely immigrant workers would be out of sight. I realized I could use this location to photograph one of these trucks, since they regularly stopped outside of the plant (these trucks never stop in public locations). Having tried, with no success, to take the photo myself with my brother and boyfriend (we were quickly kicked off the premises), I asked an acquaintance who did some work at one of these plants to take the photos for me. I got the photos, but the person who took them was fired the very next day for doing so.

These photos led to a series of paintings of animals in factory farms, including the painting of the chicken truck. Legendary artist Sue Coe has called art about animal cruelty "the kiss of death" for one's art career. I was simultaneously horrified at my newfound obsession with this topic and totally committed to working through all that I was suddenly learning and being confronted with.

During my time at Berkeley I was also meeting a lot of ex-vegetarians and being introduced to pro-meat arguments that were as ardently opposed to factory farming as I was. California was ahead of the humane meat curve, at least ahead of Georgia, as I had never heard the two words "humane" and "meat" put together before: to me it was an oxymoron. However, to many people around me humane meat made perfect sense and I was challenged in a way I hadn't ever been before to consider just what it was about eating meat, besides factory farms, that I found so unconscionable.

All I knew was that killing animals for food simply seemed wrong to me. Sure, eating an animal who had lived a contented life was better than eating an animal who had lived a tortured life, but still I thought it was cruel, especially when all the people around me who were eating these animals were privileged, middle-class individuals who certainly had countless plant foods available to them. Between my hours of painting chickens and my newfound eagerness to defend my vegetarian position, I was soon talking about these issues all the time.

And that's when it happened—the phone call from my brother Alex.

"She wouldn't ever say it to your face Sunny, but . . ." Alex paused.

"What?" I asked.

"Well, you've just been talking about being vegetarian so much, and painting that painting . . . but Sunny, those are egg-laying hens."

"Yeah . . . I guess I try not to think about that," I replied with the heaviness of someone who has been denying something important for a while.

Alex went on, "Basically, Tara just thinks you're being a bit of a hypocrite."

There is nothing like having your beloved youngest sister tell you you're being a hypocrite to make you buck up and face the facts—so that's what I did. I just started researching as much as I could—and Carol Adams' classic, *The Sexual Politics of Meat*, was one of the first books I picked up.

Through my research I found out that, indeed, the chickens I was painting were egg-laying hens, and that they were actually a different breed of chicken than the "broilers" they use for meat. I learned about the crammed spaces in which these birds live and I learned about the male chicks who are thrown away, only a day or two old, left to die slowly in the elements or as they suffocate each other. I also learned about the hens themselves, the hens like the hens I was painting, who after about a year of egg laying are slaughtered and made into ground chicken, as their bruised and debilitated bodies can't be sold for higher-priced meat. I also learned that many of these same things happen (such as the culling of male chicks and the slaughtering of "spent" hens), albeit in less gratuitously cruel ways, even on the best of small farms.

It was Adams' book, however, that helped me to consider the more theoretical questions that lay behind all of this terrible information—how does *someone* become a *something*? How are we taught to view this complete objectification of individuals as normal?

It was these questions that made me choose to become a vegan, but just as importantly that made me realize why I was a vegetarian in the first place. I realized simply that it was the objectification and exploitation of individuals that I found (and still find) so unconscionable. In other words, no matter how "humanely" animals are treated, their lives are still their own to live—they are not mine to eat.

I was at first drawn to *The Sexual Politics of Meat* for its imagery. Adams' extensive curation of images that deal with the representation of meat are still to this day some of the most powerful and complex examples of how capitalism and consumerism turn beings into products. The collection of imagery was at once witty, hilarious, and totally horrifying. It is hard to imagine how anyone could view these photographs and advertisements and not question the cultural and ethical opinions that produced them.

As I read on, it was Adams' ability to show how patriarchy affects animals that in many ways changed the direction of my work. Adams' formulation of the interconnectedness of sexism and speciesism was no doubt largely responsible for giving me the tools I needed to examine disability and animal issues as interconnected as well.

The field of disability studies has long critiqued the ways in which disability is commonly understood and represented. In her book *Contours of Ableism*, Fiona Campbell writes: "From the moment a child is born, he/she emerges into a world where he/she receives messages that to be disabled is to be *less than*, a world where disability may be *tolerated* but in the final instance, is *inherently negative*."

Ableism at its simplest is prejudice against those who are disabled and against the notion of disability itself, but more than this ableism is the historical and cultural perpetuation of discrimination and marginalization of certain bodies labeled impaired, incapable, or abnormal, and the simultaneous privileging of bodies labeled able-bodied. When we begin to consider how subjective abledness is, and how fleeting (we all go in and out of abledness as we become ill, grow older, or simply fall out of shape), we begin to understand how the dichotomy between the disabled and the able-bodied is socially constructed, and hence how the marginalization of disabled people is itself a sociopolitical phenomena. Campbell continues, "We are all, regardless of our status, shaped and formed by the politics of ableism."

Disabled people confront stereotypes, stigmas, and major civil rights infringements daily due to disability. We are the world's largest minority, the world's poorest, some of the world's least educated. The World Bank estimates that 20 percent of the world's poorest people are disabled. We are also more likely to be abused, and we are twice as likely to be victims of violence than our able-bodied friends. Disability is a social justice issue, but it's a social justice issue that Americans, and even very progressive Americans, don't really understand. Being disabled is seen as a personal problem—an individual tragedy. The problem is seen as a medical one versus a sociopolitical one.

Just as Adams presents us with how animal oppression is upheld and perpetuated by patriarchy, my work has followed in this tradition by showing how ableism is a force that also marginalizes nonhumans and justifies their continued oppression.

Given that I am someone who is female identified, *The Sexual Politics of Meat* resonated with me on a personal level as well as a theoretical level. I began to consider where the disabled body fits within these politics—bodies that are so often presented as antithetical to beauty and sexuality, bodies that are in fact often desexualized or erased altogether.

The more I looked the more I found that the disabled body is everywhere in the meat industry. The vast majority of animals we eat are themselves disabled—what I have called "manufactured to be disabled." They are mutant producers of meat, eggs, and dairy. Industrialized farm animals live in such cramped, filthy, and unnatural conditions that disabilities among them become common. In addition, they are literally bred and violently altered to physical extremes, where udders produce too much milk for a cow's body to hold, where turkeys cannot bear the weight of their own giant breasts, and where chickens are left with amputated beaks that make it difficult for them to eat.

The question I found myself asking was, Where does a disability studies analysis fit into all of this?

I have come to realize that animals, regardless of whether they are or are not disabled, are treated as inferior, devalued, and abused for many of the same basic reasons disabled people are—they are seen as incapable and different. Animals are clearly affected by the privileging of the able-bodied human ideal, which constantly is put up as the standard against which they are judged, justifying the cruelty we so often inflict upon them. From the idea that people were created in God's image, to the idea that human beings are the peek of evolution (nature's masterpiece), our anthropocentric worldview can be understood as supported and maintained by ableism. The abled body that ableism perpetuates and privileges is always not only nondisabled but also non-animal.

Animals are also affected by ableism in the form of the values and institutions it perpetuates. Ableism creates limited notions of what it means to be independent, productive, autonomous, and valuable. For example, disabled individuals are often represented as a drain on our country's resources. Instead of recognizing how interdependent we all are on each other, on our communities, and on social services, disabled people are marginalized and presented as helpless and dependent on charity. Notions of independence and productivity help form our perceptions and relationships to nonhuman animals as well, deeply affecting the way we value or devalue other animals. Ableism helps bring forth institutions and paradigms that limit our understandings of what is natural; that engender myths of normalcy; that diagnose, rank, and place value and worth on specific traits and qualities that are deemed productive, superior, profitable, and efficient. The very values, cultural norms, and institutions that perpetuate animal suffering and exploitation are born out of ableist paradigms.

Just as *The Sexual Politics of Meat* showed, more than twenty years ago, how patriarchy is an essential part of what allows animals to be seen as food, as research subjects, and as exploitable workers, my work explores how ableism is entangled with turning animals into objects for our use.

Another aspect of Adams' work that I have found to be powerful and invigorating to my own work in disability studies is the notion of the absent referent, specifically because it seemed so applicable to the ways in which disability is usually understood and represented.

The absent referent is a term used to describe the separation that occurs between the lived experiences of beings, and the objects or metaphors that they become through objectification and exploitation. The absent referent functions to erase the *someone* and turn them into a *something*. Meat is an extreme example of this separation between subject and object where literally for the meat to exist, a life had to end. The meat becomes a mass term, a generalized thing, whose meaning is severed from the individual life it once was. Throughout her books Adams describes how the absent referent functions in regards to women within a patriarchal society—how the individual lives and lived experiences of women are erased in a patriarchal culture filled with absent referents. Adams focuses specifically on pornography and the sexualization of women in advertisements and the media.

The idea of the absent referent is relevant on so many fronts and can open up avenues of recognition of what and whose bodies, exploitation, and suffering are left absent in the objects we use, the words we read, the imagery we consume and the very environments through which we move. Disability is a prime example of this.

A case in point that saturates our daily lives without most people skipping a beat is simply the use of disability as metaphor. Disability is everywhere in the English language. We say that "the economy is crippled" or say that someone is in a state of "paralysis" if they feel incapable or unable to do something. We talk of blindness as if it means ignorance or naïvety, and we describe things that we think are ignorant or unfair as "retarded."

On one level these phrases could be brushed aside as innocent metaphors and figures of speech that don't really affect the well-being of those that actually live with disabilities. But words are not apolitical.

The disability metaphors most often used whether in language or imagery are based on misrepresentations and lack of knowledge of what actual disabled people experience. The use of a word like "crippled" reinforces the idea that crippled means broken, defective, and in need of fixing. Because the word is used metaphorically, the actual lives of those who are "crippled" are both erased and simultaneously stereotyped by ideas of what "to be crippled" means. Crippled is a particularly interesting example because of the ways in which the word "crip" (which comes, of course, from cripple) has been adopted by disability scholars and activists in a similar way to how the word "queer" has been reclaimed. Like queer, crip has become an action, a way of radically altering meaning. To crip something does not mean to break it, but rather to radically and creatively invest something with a history and politics of disability history and pride, while simultaneously questioning paradigms of normalcy and medicalization.

Disability scholars realize how words reinforce how we are treated socially and politically every day, but we also realize the same is true of other kinds of representations, images, and cultural narratives. There are countless ways—from pity-mongering charity drives to sappy "super-crip" characters in movies to representations in political discourse of disabled people as scroungers, fakers, or economic burdens—in which absent referents replace the lived lives of disabled people with metaphors and stereotypes.

Hackneyed and problematic representations of disability are consistently and pervasively used as metaphors—metaphors that work to both perpetuate and justify ableism. This is true for nonhuman animals as well. Animals are not only literally objectified through absent referents, but also metaphorized. We use various animals as derogatory insults, as symbols of our bad behaviors and traits, as representation of what we don't want to be. In turn, this metaphorization contributes to and reinforces the speciesism that is used to justify their exploitation in the first place. The conceptualization of the absent referent is largely what makes *The Sexual Politics of Meat* such an important and foundational text, as it offers a simple and yet powerful tool through which to understand how objectification takes hold and how it functions in a myriad of contexts.

In various conversations I have had with people about Adams' work I have heard people criticize it for the way it could be read as depicting women simply as victims. These critics argue that in Adams' work pornography and overt sexualization are always represented as disempowering and exploitative, and that women's potential desires or choices to partake in such things are not acknowledged. People also criticize Adams' work for perpetuating heteronormative perspectives by not exploring the social construction of gender and for leaving out the experiences of queer and trans individuals. Each of these concerns would need its own dedicated focus to unpack and explore. Nonetheless, whatever critiques of Adams' work there may be in regards to these or other issues, the importance of her work on both animal rights theory and feminism cannot be denied. Her work propelled the animal rights conversation into a dialogue with feminism, challenging the male-dominated rights-based theories of conventional animal ethics while simultaneously opening the doors wide for essential intersectional work around animal liberation to take place. Similarly, Adams' work confronted feminists with the serious challenge of animal ethics, powerfully exposing the importance of exploring feminism beyond our own species.

If anyone had told me when I was first trying to take pictures of those hens for my painting that I would spend the next six years and counting examining animal oppression through a disability studies lens, I probably would have found them absurd. That original passion that first led me to ask the hard questions about why I was a vegetarian led me to Carol Adams' book. And I'm so thankful it did. *The Sexual Politics of Meat* cleared the way for animal exploitation to be examined and critiqued through analysis of intersectionality and linked oppressions, for animal issues to be seen more than ever as relevant to, even essential to, other social justice issues—including disability. It is my hope that I can add to this vital body of work by asking how the sexual politics of meat and the politics of animal ethics more generally can be cripped.

It's Not Like You Could Ever Actually Go Vegan

KATY OTTO

"*I*t's not like you could ever *actually* go vegan."

These were the words my college boyfriend said to me in the context of a fight. We were at my college dorm cafeteria and I was getting a salad. I had been vegetarian for two years, and was topping this particular salad off with egg when he looked at me antagonistically and pointed out that the same industry I protested for its killing of animals also killed and harmed animals to procure their eggs and milk. We had a contentious relationship, and I was well-versed in countering every argument he made to me—but in this case I was tongue-tied.

"You're right," I said, staring at him defiantly. "I *am* going to become vegan."

It was then that the steak-loving, beer-chugging, burger-slinging wisecrack made sure that I would never eat and drink like he did again. Though he has expressed regret and apologized in the time since, this man introduced a lot of control, abuse, and manipulation into my life when we were involved. He regularly made fun of my commitment to a cruelty-free diet.

It is hard for me to think about veganism without thinking about the book *The Sexual Politics of Meat*. In my freshman year at college, at the same time as I became vegan, I picked up a copy of Carol Adams' famous tome. I read it with fervor, knowing on an instinctual level that this book was written for people like me. I was playing music at the time, having been inspired in high school by bands like Hole, Bikini Kill, and Sleater-Kinney. I thought often of the lyrics of Kathleen Hanna, frontwoman of Bikini Kill and punk rock legend—"eat meat/hate blacks/beat your fucking wife/it's all the same thing/DENY." Yes yes yes. Through music, I was able to imagine other worlds and possibilities—to envision and organize for something different, better. The concept of taking because you could seemed sewn into the very fabric of our existence as a culture and people in the Western world. Anything gentle was shunned. Animals that we thought of as more feminine—cows, chickens, pigs—were more acceptable to kill and consume. We even had words to clean up the mess for us—such as pork, steak—that removed the animal as a subject from our minds.

It's the same when you ask your guy friend if he got any pussy, right? There isn't a person in that question. There is something to be consumed. Think of the Spur Posse, a group of young men held up as star athletes in their school who created a point-based system to score their sexual conquests. Do you think the girls they had sex with had unique personalities to them? Do you think they mattered as subjects? They mattered only in what use they were—in the same way that we can't imagine that an animal primarily raised for consumption has any worth or specialness beyond being our meal. This is a mythology, a haze that we tell ourselves so that we are desensitized, so that we are able to take flesh for what we need.

Until my freshman year of college I felt a lot of depression and unease that I couldn't name, but I didn't consider myself a feminist. I've heard this depression described by second-wave feminists as "the problem that has no name." It was related to the ceilings I saw all around me—restrictions and rules that impacted me through female socialization. I wanted an opening, some space—room to dream and create a better world. I remember from this time the sick rage I felt when I heard of friends who experienced date rape or physical abuse from boyfriends only to be slandered at school when the guy's version of the story cast blame on her. I remember holding the hand of a friend who had to go to the abortion clinic alone after her high school sweetheart got her pregnant and before her conservative father found out.

As I entered college and began taking women's studies courses, feminism ceased appearing theoretical to me. Instead, it offered tools to survive and an analysis to understand that some of the pain my friends and I experienced was not ours alone. There was a context, and there was an interrelatedness of historical systems of oppression and domination. I began taking cultural studies and race-related courses, devouring books on the labor movement and class struggle. I read *The Celling of America*, edited by Daniel Burton-Rose (a book about the prison industrial complex) and Malcolm X's autobiography on black liberation. My years in high school of working with Amnesty International and other human rights groups were leading me to question authority and systems of control. And there was no way in my heart I could understand my diet to be separate from this burgeoning discovery.

At age sixteen I became vegetarian. My family was supportive of this—my parents had been vegetarians for seven years when they were married and my sister stopped eating meat at age seven when we moved next to a butcher in southern Germany (they don't hide the source of meat in Europe as much as they do in the States, I find), my grandfather was a rare German immigrant vegetarian from childhood, and my uncle didn't eat red meat. I never had much interest in giving up my diet until one fateful Christmas. My mother's father, whom I called Papa Eff, was in our family kitchen carving up a roast beef—one of my favorites. I was watching him when he cut more than he anticipated and liquid began to spill out. He turned to my mother. "Hurry up, get a bowl! If we are fast enough we can catch all the blood and drink it or use it later."

I still remember the feeling of my heart jumping out of my chest. I was literally watching my grandfather, the head of a family with five children and nine grandchildren, scramble to "catch all the blood." I felt sick to my stomach. It was too real. I wasn't used to this much reality associated with my dinner. I stopped eating meat that night. My grandfather and grandmother were none too pleased when I told them the reason.

It's funny—I find that people do pummel you with questions about why you are vegan or vegetarian, and then express resentment, discordance, or disgust when you answer their question. This was the case with friends, acquaintances, my grandparents, and other family members. I have felt it must stem from their own instinctual discomfort with eating meat, and a desire to house that discomfort with those who have chosen differently. I don't always talk about my diet, but when you eat differently or decline certain foods consistently, you will invite conversation about it no matter what—and this I welcome. This, to me, is a powerful way to start a dialogue and plant seeds of critique. I know that in my freshman year of college as I became vegan, I was heavily inspired and assisted by two vegan women who lived next to me in the dorms. It did not hurt that they made incredible vegan cookies and were smart, driven, creative, and compassionate women (love and respect here to Christina Salvi and Miriam Heinonen).

After I read first *The Sexual Politics of Meat* and then *Animals and Women* (a breathtaking anthology edited by Carol Adams), I felt like I could sum up my veganism in a few sentences and connect it squarely with my feminist politics. I didn't want the fact that I *could* consume the body of another to mean I *did*. In fact, it struck me that this was the justification often used by those who murder, imprison, attack, abuse, or assault in order to get in the mind-set to commit such atrocities. You have to give up your belief in the body sovereignty of another being to enact violence against them. You have to disconnect from a natural sense of empathy.

I began playing music seriously at this time in my life. I wanted to carve out a space of possibility, a space in which new ideas could be amplified. In the D.C. punk community in which I'd grown up, vegetarianism, veganism, and animal rights were an integral part of the culture. Fugazi was an internationally beloved band that people traveled miles to see, and I became friends with their frontman Ian MacKaye early on in my own musical journey. He was vegan, and we had dinner parties and potlucks on occasion. I felt excited to connect with people I respected who made art and were a little older than me who had vegan diets. It was heartening to recently attend Ian's surprise fiftieth birthday party and be one of several friends curated to prepare vegan food. This mentor of mine had fifty vegan cakes to celebrate. There were a number of other vegan and vegetarian musicians in the room—people dedicated to creative practice, and to charting one's own course for ethical living.

It thrilled me to think of music inviting people into veganism, but I never felt compelled to be in a vegan band or write related lyrics myself. While I was hopeful about art as a vehicle to share ideas, my experiences weren't all positive. I heard a few songs from the infamous vegan straight-edge band Earth Crisis and went to a show of theirs, not knowing a lot about the culture of which they were a part. I found myself extremely uncomfortable and confused at this concert—here was a man, Karl Crisis, singing passionately about the sickness of factory farming and slaughter while the audience consisted mostly of guys beating each other up.

I watched some stupid things happen at this show, including a mob beating up a guy for smoking a cigarette. I couldn't get a read on whether or not the lyrics were pro-life, which also disturbed me—then, and now, I have encountered some vegan straight-edgers who equate eating meat with abortion and want to limit women's access to reproductive rights. This was not an animal rights movement I wanted to be part of. Threats to impose an animal rights agenda on others were nothing I was interested in. Those actions seemed steeped in the dynamics of coercive power and control that I was attempting to get away from in the first place. They made me move away from the vegan/straight-edge hardcore music community.

I had more personal experience with vegan/straight-edge men. My first serious relationship after college was with a guy who was vegan/straight edge. I was swept up with his passion for activism, direct action, a better world—and unable at the tender age of twenty-one to see his manipulative and abusive behaviors. We were both musicians and played in a band together; we organized actions together; we attempted to read and discuss politics together—but in the end, this vegan man, so vocal about the rights of animals, abused and harmed me and several other women. His conviction about animal rights had absolutely no bearing on his practice of empathy and his dedication to anti-oppression.

The *means* by which you inspire behavior change in another is as important if not more so than the *outcomes*. You really do need to live the change you want to see in order to be taken seriously and to inspire it in others. I wanted to make veganism appealing and exciting, and did not want to resort to cheap means to do so.

Along my journey, I was disgusted by the tactics of People for the Ethical Treatment of Animals, which included showing posters of an African American woman in a cage to evoke a slavery reference in an anti-circus campaign. I encountered this tactic my first year after college. I was working for a women and girls self-defense program, and one of our board members, herself a black woman, called me in tears after seeing such a poster in a bus station. She asked me, the only animal rights activist she knew, why this might have been a chosen strategy. I called PETA, expressing my anger at what seemed like a coarse tactic. I remember the answer of the woman who received my call distinctly:

"I took a few women's studies classes in college too. We have just chosen what we consider to be the most important agenda—animal rights—and we will use whatever tactics we can to create media attention around them."

After this I was desperate in my search for animal rights groups that had intersectional politics, however difficult they might be to find. Being vegan or vegetarian alone was not enough to live a life committed to anti-oppression politics. I discovered amazing people such as Bryant Terry, food justice activist connecting veganism with anti-racist struggle and organizing; learned about Compassion Over Killing (cok.net) and their ongoing work on specific campaigns to affect policy, while simultaneously connecting people through food-driven events and getting restaurants to include more vegan options; and visited the vegan mini-mall in Portland, Oregon. I saw that rejecting animal products could be viable, healthy, and delicious—and connected to broader social justice work.

The record label I run, Exotic Fever, was cofounded with two other women in 2000 and became a space to connect music and social justice. One of our early releases was a benefit for the D.C. area Books to Prisons Project, complete with a zine featuring prisoners' envelope artwork and essays from contributing bands on books that mattered to them. After that, Exotic Fever released benefit compilations for Vietnam Veterans of America's benefits program, HIPS (Helping Individual Prostitutes Survive), and the District Alliance for Safe Housing, a domestic violence service organization.

I decided a benefit compilation could combine music and promoting veganism in a way with which I was comfortable—through delicious recipes. We brought together sixteen artists for this release, entitled *Keep Singing!* Each artist would not only give me a song but also a vegan recipe or two to be included in a downloadable cookbook embedded on the disc. I called on a lot of musicians I had met who were themselves vegan or vegetarian, noting my desire to draw people to a vegan diet with compelling songs and welcoming dishes that were easy to prepare. My approach would be different from the vegan straight-edge hardcore scene—a scene rife with angry men. The CD, featuring a cover of beautiful, bold birds in flight, would exude hope—and would eventually raise funds for Compassion Over Killing.

Again, *tactics matter.* I wanted to think about mine. Over time, I developed a personal politic, shaped largely through the writings of women of color—and, in particular, bell hooks. These centered mostly on anti-oppression, and the refusal to subscribe to a politics of domination in its many manifestations and forms. I learned how factory farming was shaped by capitalism—driven by the gospel that you had to produce as quickly and as much as possible. I realized animal products other than meat were obtained through the exploitation of another creature's reproductive functionality—milk and eggs. Capitalism rears its head to control reproduction for financial gain. More workers, more eggs, more milk. More suffering.

Unfortunately, through my participation in the animals rights movement I have met a number of male-identified folks who do not in any way challenge their sexist assumptions—some of whom develop a reputation of coercive or manipulative behavior, some of whom let the bulk of organizing work fall to women in their ranks, and so forth. One man in particular, a noted animal rights activist, had a Facebook profile at one point with an array of different women at his side, staring up at him adoringly after his release from prison for what was actually a strategically ineffective animal rights action. From my experiences traveling as a touring musician, I began to hear stories of this particular man's various stints staying on the couches of vegan women animal rights activists rent-free. I guess in some way, they were his absent referents. One woman told me he never was forthright with her about his other lovers.

Music introduced me to another vegan artist—my friend Tom Gabel of the band Against Me!, who has since transitioned into a woman, very publicly and bravely, and is now named Laura Jane Grace. Ethical diet was something we bonded over when we met and became friends. Laura expressed to me recently in an email a desire to connect with other trans folks who were vegan, because hormone replacement therapy requires some diet adjustments that make veganism nearly impossible. She has had to make changes, but in my mind her belief in animal rights remains integral.

It is imperative in speaking about sexual politics today to include engaged dialogue about transgender inclusion. In fact, a lot of transphobia calls upon the same evocation of an absent referent—hateful terms like "she-male" or "he-she" which offer nothing about an individual or their struggles and strengths. In a recent article in *Rolling Stone,* my beautiful friend Laura spoke about not wanting to be seen as "the sad tranny." This sharp image is alive in public imagination because we have subscribed to absent reference. Adams speaks in her book about how language serves to police. It sets a cultural standard and finds ways to let you know you don't fit. There is no way my friend could ever be seen this way in the world, as "sad"—it simply isn't possible, given her talent, voice, vitriol, and passion. But even the notion of a "sad tranny" is a fiction. It helps to separate us, enable dehumanization, and facilitate violence. Celebrating transgender people in our world is also a way of honoring body sovereignty. It is standing firm with the notion that people deserve to have control over their own bodies, and that this control needs to be respected. In fact, transgender people are opening up space bravely and creatively, for all of us to live more freely from their own imagined sense of self. As far as I am concerned, transgender activism is the next step in the roadmap laid out in Adams' book.

The Sexual Politics of Meat is one of what will hopefully be many works on how anti-oppression politics overlap, and on how to live based on those politics. We need to know that refusing to eat meat can be an example of a new kind of ethical masculinity. We need voices and stories of men who reject the dominant narrative. We need to not equate consuming meat with strength. We need to embrace the end of a gender binary. We need to make veganism inviting and interesting. It is a creative way to live. It is a rejection of the status quo and an assertion that just because things are a certain way does not mean they should be. It is a daily path that can open up possibility—but if it is not conducted in tandem with ongoing critique of one's own complicity in oppression, capitalism, sexism, racism, homo/transphobia—then it isn't any politic that interests me at all. Carol Adams' book and her work challenged me at age eighteen to try a little harder—and at thirty-three, I am so glad she did. Living a vegan life helps remind me each day that what I do on earth matters, and that no matter how small an action to resist and refuse domination may seem, it can have impact.

Oh, and by the way—my college boyfriend co-owns a sausage stand now. It would never have worked out.

Girl

Teenage Wasteland

KATE LARSON

*C*arol Adams has said a lot of things better than I ever will, but that does not mean I have not tried to say things anyway. Most of the time I try to forget about everything she's said. Sometimes I try to paint over it all, tuck it away, pretend it's not even there, because it's too damn hard to live knowing these things. It's too hard to press on in spite of it.

You can see any culture working by looking at the kids. You can see the evidence. My culture took it out of me. My culture helped me take it out of myself. I hate to tell this story, to even bring up teenage eating disorders. Has there ever been a teenage girl who didn't have an eating disorder? Is this the new standard? Is it just assumed? Is it being taken seriously? No one seems surprised anymore. We all can understand where it's coming from, where it's rooted itself in us. I'd like to think that I know better, that I've always known better, because it all sounds so useless. It feels so shameful and tired to have to confess these things, to draw them out. The truth is, I haven't always known better, and it is not my fault.

I feel like I shouldn't really blame my culture, but the evidence is there, it's here, it's all over myself, streaming down my front, lingering, leaving a stain. I'm not alone in it, although I wish I were. I stopped eating in high school because I didn't think it was worth it. I stopped caring about anything else besides what of me was being shed, and it was never enough. Tired, textbook story—girls hate themselves. It is not shocking to see the statistics and it's really a damn shame. No one is stunned at the figures. No one is asking "But why?" We all get it. Girls continue to fade off, disappear, wage war.

Whole girls boil down to these eating disorders, and the disorders sieve off into three-letter pet names. Anorexia becomes "Ana," bulimia becomes "Mia." The brutal lifestyle and daily trials of restricting and purging are now girl names. Innocent and short. Names to hang onto, to fuse with. I did so with fervor. I had a red bracelet with block bead letters spelling "ANA," and I could get away with this. For all anyone knew, Ana was simply a friend. Perhaps we missed each other. Perhaps this bracelet was a good way to keep her close, to make sure I didn't forget her. It was all true: the obsession becomes another member of your family, another part of you, a new limb to drag around. But it wasn't as harmless as the girl names suggest. Ana was a hellish friend. She wore away at me. We wore away together.

I went vegetarian at a young age, inspired by a great pang in my gut, a flash in my brain, a moral conscience quickly developing, expanding its size. I was attuned to animal cruelty in sixth grade, boycotting all companies with which it was associated. I drove my mother up a wall in the process—a simple item on my school supplies list like Post-it notes would warrant a weeklong search for a company that did not test their glue on laboratory animals. I knew of Proctor and Gamble's history of unapologetic animal testing, and I carried around a list of the companies they owned, determined to keep their products from my mother's shopping cart. I was admittedly a brat: I had serious convictions and more serious self-discipline. Unfortunately, I also applied this to anorexia. I was ruthless. It started out simple: I only wanted to lose a little weight. I just wanted to pare some pieces of me down. The method I chose was restricting, and then it ballooned out, losing sight of me. It happened suddenly. I learned the tricks, and I hung onto them tightly. Apple cider vinegar is rumored to speed up metabolism. Ankle weights and baggy pants combine to help fake bulk at weigh-ins at the doctor. Alternating caloric intakes slightly every day in a pattern can keep you from reaching a plateau weight. And there is *always* the option to purge. A "thinspiration" notebook filled with magazine-torn photographs of thin models functioned as a daily reminder of what I was doing all this for. The excuse "I'm just not hungry" can go a long way. Veganism helped: there was often not something that I could eat. Some fruits and vegetables burn more calories digesting than they give you. My body stopped menstruating under these circumstances. I wasn't giving myself the things I needed to function and grow, and it gave up on me. In my stupor, I saw this as a bonus. I was afraid of myself.

As I went vegan, my relationship with Ana got more serious. I looked at the spread at the dinner table and abruptly said "No more," pushing away the butter and milk. My mother's face glowed in shock, unprepared. What would I eat? Would my bones collapse? Would I blow away? Silly concerns now, but fairly apt ones in retrospect. Shortly thereafter I began to look at every plate, saying "No more." I treated myself as undeserving. I shut out lots of foods on their basis of "not being vegan," but it was also just a plain, clear-cut excuse not to eat. I cared about the animals: the politics, the oppression, the karma and conscience. But I didn't care about myself. I couldn't connect the dots.

Sexism gets deep inside of us. Body shaming wraps itself around our limbs, clings tight and contracts. We see it and we learn it. We police each other, we police ourselves, and it's wrong, it's a useless pursuit. It never mattered that I knew that killing animals was not a noble act, it didn't matter that I fought against the tide. I couldn't make the bigger connection. I couldn't see that I wasn't getting anywhere in my own body, trying to survive while trying to disappear. Scraping by as means to success. Habits die hard and when they're learned young, even more so. The art of restricting—denying myself some basic needs and sustenance, *was* my main sustenance. It was my focus, a reason to wake up in the morning. Hating myself so much that each day was a glimmering shot at fixing it—to see how little I could take in without passing out and losing myself completely—to see how strong I really was, underneath. It was exhilarating to teeter on the line. It felt like brilliant success to still be standing at the end of each hard-won day. No one ever tells you and you'd never guess, though, that it's impossible to ever feel you've done enough, like you've lost enough weight. You'll never start liking yourself when in this cycle. You'll waste away, or you'll eventually fight back.

It all starts simple enough and hopefully it ends the same. Women all see that we're not valued, not good enough, unless we look the part, unless we shut up or shut down. We learn this, hold it so deeply inside of ourselves that we can't even see it at all. It takes some decent work to claw out. In the midst of anorexia, I didn't value my own livelihood, but I valued the livelihood of others. I went vegan because of this care, this concern. I did it and it hadn't even occurred to me to see how starkly it stood next to my treatment of my own body.

I am proud for still standing today. I know that my culture didn't care when I fell for its traps, and I know it also didn't care when I said "Enough." I know I'm just part of a massive statistic, another number to add and subtract to the reports. I feel like I've won something, though. I've torn a virus from my body. I stand here because a doctor saw through to the other side of me, because she gave me some words to toss around in my mouth. I'm here because one friend confronted me, she spoke up, and then another friend did the same. I was scared of what would happen to me if I kept going, but I was just as scared of what would happen to me if I stopped, if I lost that focus, that identity, that friend Ana. I was lucky enough to take a step back, to be able to gain focus in the fog. I decided that I couldn't do it anymore. To put an incredibly intensive process rather simply: I slowly taught myself how to eat again, how to live. I began to sweep up the fractions of myself. When they took form, I pushed myself up. I found the way out.

Years after my battle, my father approached me at a family reunion to tell me how much he really appreciated it when I had lost all that weight, years back. He was never present enough in my life to understand what was happening to me, why I was losing weight, shrinking size, shedding myself. He could only tell me that he is grateful that I did, thinking that I would take it as a compliment. This painted a nice picture for me of the bottom line, what women go through to keep up appearances, and how they are rewarded by everyone else. How "thin" has washed out all the other standards, how happy we are to see people when they're skinny, when they may be losing themselves. How we don't ask questions, how we maybe don't want to hear the answers. I didn't know what I could have possibly said to him in response. I didn't say anything at all.

There are things I do now that only make sense to me when they are magnified, when held up against my former self. Spending four hours cooking a meal for myself that takes minutes to eat,. Finding communion in potlucks, in the sharing of food. Resolving to love every single fold of myself. Never counting a single calorie, never letting my size dictate my self-worth. Resolving to bid adieu to anyone in my life who tries to push me back into the muck. Food carves out such a big space in my life now because of its huge absence so many years ago. I'm so grateful to still be here to consider, eat, and enjoy it. I have come out alive, I have come out stronger, and I can advocate for the bodies and lives of women and animals because of it. These things keep me thankful. They keep me in motion. These things are interchangeable to me right now.

Happy Rape, Happy Meat

DALLAS RISING

*W*hen I was fifteen years old, I was raped by a twenty-two-year-old. It wasn't a back-alley or home-invasion style rape. He didn't drag me kicking and screaming to the floor. He didn't hold a knife to my throat or a gun to my head. In fact, like many rape victims, I had consented to kissing him and letting him touch me. But at a certain point, I realized that he wasn't interested in whether or not I was consenting.

I had just met this guy a few hours prior. My mom had dropped me off at a hotel for a science fiction and comic conference and I had no friends waiting for me there, though I had led her to believe I did. When I was a teenager I never thought I felt invincible, but looking back at the events of that night, I understand why so many adults claim teens feel precisely that. At one point I must have thought it would be fun to go and knew that I wouldn't have been allowed to go alone, so I hatched a plan. However, when push came to shove, I felt uneasy about going alone. Unfortunately, I had a bad habit of changing my mind at the last minute. When I tried to get out of going, my mom decided that this time she wasn't going to rearrange her schedule and plans to accommodate my whims. Unwilling to admit that I had lied and was losing my nerve, my mom was under the assumption that once she dropped off her sullen teenage daughter at the door, I would walk inside, meet up with my friends, and have a great time. It was one of her tough love moves, and if I had told her the truth, I'm sure that things would have gone exactly as she'd predicted. But I had lied to her and made the choice to cover that lie, so they didn't go that way at all.

She let me know what time she'd be back to get me in the morning and dropped me off in front of the glass doors of the huge building. Of course, if she had had any idea what would happen to me just hours from the time she dropped me off, she never would have left me there. I remember feeling a low level of anxiety and fear, wishing that I was still in the car with her as she drove off instead of being left here amid strangers. I didn't have a room to stay in, so I had no safe space to retreat to. I ended up wandering the carpeted halls and riding escalators up and down the mezzanine, ducking in and out of workshops that held no interest for me, looking for someplace where I could be unobtrusive and out of the way for a while.

When I was fifteen years old, I wore fishnets and combat boots, short skirts and dark lipstick. I was a child trying to look tough, which just highlighted my vulnerability. I used to clomp down the streets in my boots, walking with intention and blaring Nine Inch Nails through my headphones, but this night I had nowhere to go. Today I regularly assist with women's self-defense workshops, and one of the first things we teach is that predators look for easy targets, so don't look like an easy target: walk briskly, stay alert, and exude a general confidence and a don't-fuck-with-me vibe. Looking back on that night, I understand exactly how I was singled out by this predator.

I was young and obviously alone. As the night wore on I became more and more tired and struggled to stay alert. I was lonely and exhausted and just wanted to go home. The effort of looking like I wasn't alone and lost was wearing me down. I was terribly vulnerable and the very definition of an easy target. Not realizing any of this, only knowing that I wanted badly to go home, I called my mom and asked her if she would come and get me early. She held her ground, still thinking that I was safe and just in a sour mood. She would be there in the morning, she assured me, but not before the stated collection time. I remember feeling weak and embarrassed for being afraid to be on my own for one night at fifteen years old. It wasn't like I was on the streets or anything; I was in a hotel with a bunch of weirdos in Star Trek costumes. Nerds like that don't fit the predator/rapist stereotype.

As I walked past some ground-level rooms with sliding glass doors, a group of young men called out some mean and demeaning comments to me. I don't remember what they said, but I do remember feeling close to tears already from exhaustion and loneliness and whatever they shouted out made me angry on top of those other emotions. I ignored them and just kept walking, looking for a corner where I could curl up and wait out the remaining hours of the night.

I kept walking, but one of the guys from the group came up behind me and tapped me on the shoulder. "I'm sorry my friends are such jerks," he said. "They can be really immature sometimes. Are you okay?" Immediately I thought that this was a nice guy: he showed he wasn't the same as his friends, he expressed concern for me, and he implied that he and I were the mature ones, not his idiot friends. I was so desperate for someone to connect with that I welcomed his invitation to hang out and talk.

As we talked he continued to look for ways to identify with me and me with him. He was a friendly face in a sea of strange strangers (I quickly forgot that he, too, was a stranger). He wasn't in a weird costume, and he looked like an average college kid and was not only paying attention to me, but being nice. I thought I had made a friend. A much-needed friend.

When he "realized he'd forgotten something at his apartment," he asked me if I'd like to tag along with him while he ran home to get it. Eager to get away from the place where I had felt uncomfortable for hours, I agreed. I remember walking to his car in the lot and the sun was coming up. It was a relief that I only had a few more hours until my mom would come to get me.

He drove us to his apartment, which was located a just few miles down the road on the same street where I lived. I was within walking distance of my house. I felt safer in an area I recognized, knowing exactly how to get home. He brought me up to his studio apartment, and the place was a mess. I remember looking around and seeing there was nowhere to sit but on his bed. He had me sit down there while he dug around looking for whatever it was he had forgotten. But of course it didn't take long for him to make it to the bed and start kissing me.

I remember feeling really strange and out of it. I was so tired that my ability to think clearly was impaired. I felt a misguided sense of strength in rebellion, making out with an older guy I'd just met, in his apartment, when I was fifteen and only hours before had called my mommy to come and get me because I was too scared to be alone all night with strangers. I thought I had turned a corner and was suddenly becoming independent and mature. So I let him take off my clothes.

When he reached for a condom I got nervous. I had never had sex before and I didn't know this guy. *Oh shit, I don't know this guy! What am I doing half naked in his bed? What is happening?* I felt drugged with sleep deprivation and suddenly very afraid. *What am*

I going to do? I hardly had enough energy to keep my eyes open, let alone run down the street. *Where are my clothes?* I had lied and told him I was sixteen. *Is this my fault? Do I deserve this for lying and trying to be someone I'm not?*

While all of these thoughts were going through my head, he'd put his yellow condom-covered dick in me and was pawing and moaning and I wanted to throw up. The tattoo on his arm that I'd thought was so cool a few minutes ago seemed sinister and evil. The sun, which I had seen as a sign of hope less than an hour before, felt like an illumination of my shame. I looked out the window and saw that familiar intersection and wanted to weep.

But I didn't. When he was done, he got up and put on his clothes and said we had to hurry because his friends were waiting. The same friends he'd distanced himself from before were now the important ones and I needed to hurry to accommodate the people who had verbally abused me earlier. He didn't ask me if I was okay. He didn't hold me or tell me I was special. He just insinuated that I was going to make him late. He had more important things on his mind than my experience. Maybe he hurried so that he wouldn't have to be present with what he'd done to me.

When my mom picked me up and I got in the house, she looked at me and said, "You had sex, didn't you?" and while I understand that I heard her through a veil of shame and trauma, she didn't sound concerned or happy about it. She sounded disappointed. Annoyed. Disgusted. I felt the sour rot of shame all through my gut. Like the biggest fuck-up in the world. And at the same time, I was furious with her because I had called and asked her to come and get me, hadn't I? But I didn't say any of that. I couldn't get much out between my body-racking sobs, but I managed to explain enough. I don't remember much about that morning, but my mom says I refused to allow her to call the police. I am sure this is because I was afraid she would find out I had lied to her, and that I was partially at fault for lying about my age, too. Shame engulfed me.

My demeanor prior to the rape was silly, outspoken, and full of humor. But for a long time afterward I just wanted to hide, like a traumatized cat who seems never to come out from under the bed. I proceeded to skip classes and go from A's and B+'s to C's and D-'s by final exams. I couldn't pay attention in school, I became depressed and started my on-and-off relationship with self-injury. I withdrew and continued to blame myself for being stupid while at the same time becoming more promiscuous with boys (though being careful never to have vaginal intercourse) in an attempt to feel some level of control and desirability. I started telling boys to stop when I was really ready to fight them, to test them and see if they listened.

It took me seven years, until I was twenty-two years old and could look at fifteen-year-olds with some distance, to realize that I had been singled out long before my rapist stopped listening to me in his bed. He had set me up before I'd even seen his face. It's now been seventeen years since my rape and I still cry about it. I get pissed because I have done all the work I can think to do about it. I no longer feel like it was my fault. I've done all the therapy and I fully understand what happened and how it happened. I wish that meant that I could stop hurting or feeling pain around it, but it still hurts. And it very likely will for the rest of my life.

AS ANIMAL LIBERATIONISTS continue to educate the public about the realities of animal farming, agribusiness has done an excellent job capitalizing on the sympathy most people have for animals and the desire that flesh eaters have to remain in denial about the impact their actions have on others. "Happy meat" is marketed to such a degree that many people feel not only comfortable but *good* about buying products marketed as "humane," "grass-fed," "free-range," "humane certified," and so on. As an abolitionist animal liberationist, I am busier than ever combating the humane farming myth and working to minimize damage done not only by animal-abusing industries, but several so-called animal advocacy groups who are now partnering with these industries to create new ways to raise and kill animals that will be less offensive to people who purport to care about animals.

One of the most effective ways that I have to explain why I don't support, condone, or encourage anyone to buy "happy meat" is by comparing it to rape. And this analogy has made some people pretty angry.

When I am in a situation where I need to explain the moral difference between "happy meat" and conventionally factory-farmed meat, I have taken to using a rape analogy, and this has made some other animal activists angry. I have been known to say, "Promoting happy meat or cage-free eggs is like working to get rapists to rape without holding guns or knives to their victims' throats. Anyone can recognize that that's an absurd tactic and any group taking that approach would be vilified (and rightfully so). But so-called animal advocacy groups do it all the time and people love them for it. Why not actually work for what we believe is right and be clear about what we want: an end to the unnecessary violence and violations perpetrated on animals daily."

I use this analogy because there is a widely held cultural agreement that rape is an unnecessary violence and no one should ever be the victim of this kind of violence. I feel it helps expose violence toward nonhuman animals for what it is: unnecessary violence. It helps me illustrate a vital point: violence is violence, no matter who the victim is.

But I have gotten mail from some women who feel I have crossed a line by using rape to argue against animal abuse. They contend that while both animals and women are victimized in our society, they are victimized in different ways. They say that differences in legality as well as how the histories of these two types of violence and the way they're viewed culturally all make my using rape as a way to talk about animal abuse unacceptable. I have been told that "tossing the word rape around" cheapens the experiences of both nonhuman animal victims as well as the human victims of rape. I've been reprimanded for risking triggering a rape survivor by using the word *rape,* thereby allowing my listener to dismiss what I have to say or take offense and become unwilling to hear me out, not to mention unnecessarily re-traumatizing any could-be rape survivors.

And while I trust that the women who wrote to me are only trying to give me a constructive critique, I kind of want to scream. Because this is exactly how I see this issue, keeping in mind that I am, myself, a survivor of "happy rape." I wasn't accosted in a dark alley by a man with a knife, raped, beaten, and left for dead. My story is much different than that. I worried for years that it was my fault because my rape didn't look like that. But it was still rape and it was still wrong and it still left me traumatized and wounded. Hearing people advocate for cage-free eggs or asking people to go vegetarian instead of vegan when they know the violence inherent in the dairy and egg industries is, to me, exactly like hearing that my rape doesn't count. I wasn't violated to the degree that they feel is sufficient to be worth speaking out against.

And what about me as a survivor? Does the fact that those kinds of actions and comments remind me of my own pain not count? As someone who has lived with the aftermath of rape for seventeen years, being accused of throwing the word around lightly doesn't sit well with me. And what about the implied criticism of using an emotional topic (rape) to address an emotional topic (violence inflicted upon vulnerable animals)? Isn't that a misogynistic value system, where women are often accused of being overly emotional and hysterical when it comes to animal issues?

I was raped when I was fifteen, and that's also when I went vegan. For years I had guilt and shame when I would start to enjoy my sexuality too much. If I let myself feel too good sexually, my brain would interrupt it with images of foxes being electrocuted and skinned, or pigs hanging upside down by one shackled foot, kicking for their lives while their blood splashed onto a concrete floor below them. Depending on how well I knew my partner, I would either break down and cry or stuff it down and not. From a very early age, sex and victimization, of both myself and nonhuman animals, have been intertwined for me.

As animal advocates we are often accused of valuing animal lives over human lives. I wonder if some people are so afraid of coming across with that bias that they flip too far to the other side. Have we gotten so wrapped up in the political correctness of women's studies jargon that we're no longer willing to listen to a woman whose views differ from our own, and in attempting to defend a large theoretical group of imaginary "women" we miss the very real experience of the woman we are interacting with in that moment? I see this as no different from the disassociation that infects our movement when we refer to "the animals" as though there is such an entity as all of the animals. There isn't. There are just billions of individual animals living independent lives with unique feelings, experiences, and desires. Let's not get so wrapped up in academia, ideology, theory, and women's studies jargon that we lose sight of the fact that these are living, breathing, feeling individuals we're talking about.

Another issue I have with the people who accuse me of taking unnecessary risks that may upset some people is that they assume that anyone has the right not to be upset. That's bogus. Of course, if we can avoid causing unnecessary harm, that is what we ought to do. People have a right not to be raped. They do *not* have a right to never be upset due to someone talking about rape in a way in which they disapprove.

The fact is that we are talking about painful issues and there is no getting around the fact that these things hurt. Being raped hurts. Being reminded of your rape hurts. Having your reproductive choices taken away from you hurts. Having your babies taken away from you hurts. It doesn't matter if the victim is human or not. It doesn't matter if the violence occurs in the nineteenth century or the twentieth century. It doesn't matter if the victim is the legal property of the perpetrator or not. It's all painful.

As a movement we need to model how to deal head-on with issues that are painful to examine, think about, and talk about, because perpetrators of violence gain power when their actions are kept hidden or silent. And if someone is triggered by that sort of discussion, then it's our job to support them as they work through that pain and start making the connections between the violence done to women and violence done to nonhuman animals.

Horse

Queering the Dinner Table

MARGARET PERRET

*L*ike much of middle-class America, my family obses-
sively maintained a semblance of "family values": my parents
insisted that the four of us—my mom, dad, sister, and I—sit down
for a meal together every night around six o'clock. My mom would
cook dinner, set the table, and then call us to eat meals that typically
consisted of a rice or pasta dish, vegetables, and a large chunk of
meat. We would sit down, hold hands, and say a prayer, and then
my dad would comment on the food. If the meal consisted of meat
he liked, he would say "Looks good, Debbie." If there was no meat,
however, he would ask, "Where's the meat?", often with a mocking
smile on his face. At this point, my mom would either leave the table,
offended, or ignore his comment and eat in silence. Depriving my
dad of meat always ruined a meal.

Eventually, my parents' marriage fell apart and they divorced
during my mid-teenage years. As we sat in a California Pizza Kitchen,
my dad tried to explain to me why they were getting divorced. While
there were larger problems in their marriage, part of his explanation
was what he saw as my mom's reluctance to perform domestic labor.

"Your mother didn't want me anymore. She always resented the cooking and cleaning."

I cringed. "If she didn't want to do housework, then she shouldn't have to!"

"That was the way I was raised. The woman takes care of the house and the kids."

Indignant, I said, "I'm certainly not going to be a slave for some man."

Taking a bite of his pizza and leaning back in his chair, my dad replied, "Well, I guess you don't *have* to do all the housework, but you have to tell whatever guy you're going to marry about it beforehand because he might not be okay with it."

"So, you're getting a divorce because you didn't want to pick up a broom?"

"That's the woman's job. No man is supposed to do that kind of thing. The man gets a job and is the provider. That's the way my parents did it and the way I've always wanted it."

In that moment, as I watched my dad eat his pizza stacked with pepperoni and sausage, my mind flashed to the fights over meatless dinners. In my home, meat eating was wrapped up in politics of dominance, masculinity, and subjectivity.

Masculinity in Western culture is predicated, in part, on the ability to dominate animals though killing them for food and women through control of their bodies. Masculine control of both nonhuman animals' and women's bodies together suggest an assumed right to be served and eat animal flesh. Because meat is a symbol of male dominance, removing meat from the table queers the power relations that traditionally structure our meals. Therefore, whether consciously or unconsciously, women who do not serve meat to men defy the patriarchal structure by insisting on both their own subjectivity and the subjectivity of animals that are killed for food. For my dad and, more inclusively, men in modern Western societies, institutionalizing meat eating is a way to maintain patriarchal values and, by extension, male privilege.

I became a vegetarian during my first year in high school, in the midst of this familial conflict over meat eating. On Tuesdays, Wednesdays, and Thursdays, after I got out of school, my aunt Amy and I would drive together to the Paddock Riding Club to visit our horses Adriano and Astro Boy. One afternoon, while we were stuck in traffic on the 5 Freeway, Aunt Amy told me that she was reading the book *Skinny Bitch* and considering vegetarianism.

"It's really disgusting. I can't believe I've been putting all this junk in my body." She reached in the side compartment of her car and handed me the book.

I stared at the cover with the words *Skinny Bitch* written in big, glaring letters and a sketch of an impossibly skinny woman with a waist the width of her forearms. Enough to make any feminist shudder. I decided not to politicize our conversation. "So, what should we be eating?"

"It has some great advice—organic veggies, fruit, nuts, whole grains. It's simple, really."

Surprised, I asked, "No meat? Isn't fish and chicken supposed to be really healthy?"

"Look at Chapter Four. Apparently meat makes us fat."

"'Chapter Four: The Dead, Rotting, Decompsing Flesh Diet,'" I read.

Aunt Amy laughed. "That's what meat really is! We are making our bodies graveyards."

"I guess I just never thought of it that way."

"Yeah, it's so gross. Animals live in their own filth and are pumped full of hormones and chemicals. And our bodies can't digest meat properly so it's really unhealthy. And vegetarians are way less likely to be fat than people who eat meat. . . ."

Aunt Amy chattered on, but I was only half listening. *Meat is animal flesh? Animals are killed for me to eat meat? I love animals. Why would I want to kill them?*

Before that afternoon, I did not know anyone who was a vegetarian or was considering a vegetarian lifestyle, so I really had no concept of the possibility of not eating meat. I had never thought seriously about where my food came from, and certainly did not realize that my mom's homemade hamburgers came from an animal that was hauntingly similar to my precious horse, Adriano. That night I googled "factory farms" and clicked on a YouTube video entitled "Factory Farm Animal Cruelty," which was a compilation of video clips from undercover animal cruelty investigations. I saw struggling, terrified chickens hung by their ankles on the slaughterhouse conveyor belt, a gang of factory farm workers repeatedly striking a pig's head with a concrete block, and the frightened eyes of a cow that was being butchered alive. Aunt Amy was telling the truth. I never touched meat again.

While at the time I attributed my dietary change to a moral epiphany, it would be disingenuous to say that my food choices were not partially a response to what I perceived to be the gender politics in my home and Western culture. It is telling that I was introduced to elementary feminist theory just before becoming a vegetarian, and with these theoretical tools I became aware of the prevalence of gender inequities. I was horrified to realize that I was growing up in a world where domestic violence, objectification, rape, and war were expected parts of the female experience. My response to patriarchal domination mirrored the way I felt when I discovered the fate of nonhuman animals in the slaughterhouse. The gendered conflict over meat in my home—in addition to my rejection of the patriarchal values of domination, violence, and aggression—helped shape my vegetarianism, much like it did for many women in Carol Adams' book.

The Sexual Politics of Meat helped me realize that my choice of vegetarianism had both moral and historical continuity with women of the past. Carol Adams' research on vegetarianism in women's movements throughout history shows us that there is a precedent for vegetarianism among progressive women. Food, Adams argues, is an essential part of an individual's identity, particularly for women, and "going vegetarian" has historically been a result of increased self-awareness and/or dissatisfaction with gender inequalities. Learning about the connections of historical feminists to vegetarianism produced a greater context for helping me understand that in choosing ethical vegetarianism, I am also choosing feminism. My experience, then, demonstrates how food can be a place where privilege, gender politics, and morality are both contested and maintained.

Several years later, my veganism grew out of increasingly radical, anti-establishmentarian politics. At the same time, I was introduced to radical feminist theory, including queer theory, post-Marxist analysis and, perhaps most notably, theories of intersectionality. But it was through *The Sexual Politics of Meat* that I began to make the connections. In particular, the notion of the absent referent revolutionized what I saw as the interdependency of radical feminism and animal liberation.

One of the leading reasons for my veganism, and one of the most direct intersections between women's oppression and animal exploitation, is that female animals are doubly exploited for both their flesh and reproductive capacities. In the meat, egg, and dairy industries, female animals become oppressed by their biological capacities as mothers. Undoubtedly, milk production for human consumption is violence against the female reproductive system and sanctity of motherhood; thus, the "rape rack" enables and defends a world of rapists. If we recognize the intersection between women's oppression and the dairy and meat industries, then it is clear that to overthrow the literal and figurative patriarchal consumption of non-human animals and women, we must stop the violence against the female reproductive system that occurs in the meat, eggs, and dairy industries.

The summer I picked up *The Sexual Politics of Meat* was also when my queerness became a more important part of my identity. Although not explicitly stated in the book, by inference it is clear that the men who most vehemently defend meat eating and are threatened by women-identified dietary choices are often those most violently opposed to homosexuality and non-normative gender expression. Masculinity predicated on sexual aggression and a commitment to meat eating function together to construct an assumed male heterosexuality. The result is that relations to meat eating encode both gender expression and sexual identity. Thus, vegetarians are often called "fags" and tofu is considered "gay." When vegetarians and vegetarian-identified foods are verbally linked with homosexuality, the speaker makes a value judgment where both vegetarianism and homosexuality are seen as feminizing, illegitimate, unnatural, and even sinful.

I remember one humorous conversation with a male acquaintance regarding this very issue. We were in the midst of discussing food sovereignty for communities of color in Los Angeles when I said, "A true democratic food system would have to be decentralized, vegan, and organic."

Missing the point, he blurted out, "Yeah, that all sounds good and I like soymilk, but I don't eat or drink soy because it would give me man-boobs and make me gay."

"Do you seriously think that soy can make someone gay?"

"Someone sent me an article about female hormones in soy or something like that. I'm not sure if it's true, but I avoid it just in case."

"There are *estrogen-like* compounds in soy, called plant estrogens. But they're in such low concentrations that it is highly, highly doubtful that they could give you 'effeminate' features such as 'man-boobs.' And there is absolutely no scientific evidence to suggest that eating soy can make a person gay."

It is telling that while beer, meat from soy-fed animals, and soy products all contain estrogen-like compounds, it is assumed that drinking soymilk feminizes males, while drinking beer and eating meat does not. Not only does this example illustrate the saliency of the somewhat illogical mythology surrounding meat eating but, more alarmingly, it draws on the assumption that "real" masculinity is by necessity heterosexual and, by extension, femininity and homosexuality are undesirable, unnatural, even freakish. Dietary taboos surrounding soy products illustrate the sometimes subtle, but always damaging, homophobia and transphobia in patriarchal cultures.

The Sexual Politics of Meat and other scholarly works on gender and sexuality are important because they allow young, queer vegans to identify the structures and cultural dynamics that reinscribe homophobia, sexism, and animal oppression. Once identified, these structures and cultural dynamics can be contested and changed. Women who are romantically involved with women or who eat plant-based diets similarly deny masculinist, meat-eating culture by disrupting structures of violence that both reaffirm a dominant masculinity predicated on a lack of empathy and perpetuate the subjugation of women and nonhuman animals. As a queer vegan, I am doubly resisting structures of violence and oppression in modern Western society by rejecting patriarchal control of my body and the bodies of nonhuman animals. By embracing queerness or choosing to be queer-allied, we can rebel against part of a hierarchy that values masculinity over femininity, heterosexuality over homosexuality, and human bodies over animal ones. *The Sexual Politics of Meat* has helped me see that whom I eat and whom I love are places for feminist resistance.

Since embracing a queer-vegan lifestyle, there have been many times when my life choices have been contested and discredited. For example, as my girlfriend Kelsey and I walked past a group of four older men in downtown San Francisco, one of them commented, "Damn. I want to fuck these girls."

"We aren't objects for your sexual pleasure," I snapped.

He laughed with his friends, gestured in my direction, and exclaimed, "Looks like the aggressive one needs the dildo!"

In first ignoring our relationship and then assuming that it resembled a heterosexual one, he dismissed the legitimacy of the relationship and, by extension, all women participating in non-heterosexual relationships.

This was not an isolated incident. I have received many comments about my inability as a woman to please my girlfriend; questions about if I am the "man" or "woman" in relationships; assumptions that my girlfriend and I would be thrilled to have a man with us in bed; offers to beat up my assumed "butch girlfriend at home" so that I could be with a man; and because of my more feminine gender expression, backhanded compliments about how I do not "look gay" or am "too pretty" to be gay.

These comments are not so different from the responses to my veganism: "Are you really a vegan?" "Are you always a vegan?" "But meat eating is natural! Lions eat meat!" "Plants have feelings, too! Isn't it cruel to eat them?" "Do you like animals more than people?" "Do you mind if I already put bacon pieces in the green beans?" "I eat meat because it tastes good!" "Vegans are always so sickly looking" "Would you eat meat if you were on a desert island and you'd starve to death if you didn't?" and "I think some animals want to be eaten." I have found that comments about my queerness and veganism reflect queerphobia and veganphobia in patriarchal culture, respectively.

Adams presents several theoretical insights into why verbal attacks against LGBTQQIA people and vegans are structurally determined in a similar way in a patriarchal society. Perhaps most striking is the observation that both fail to take seriously the ethical, political, and personal dimensions of a vegan or queer lifestyle. Trivializing and delegitimating, verbal attacks against LGBTQQIA people and veg*ns (meaning both vegans and vegetarians) are attempts to disempower the reformer and uphold Western, patriarchal hierarchies. It is clear that responses to my veganism are not earnest efforts to understand the theoretical and moral basis for my dietary choices, but rather teasing manipulations, as indicated by ludicrous questions about the sentience of plants, the legitimacy of carnivorous animals, or the stringency of my dietary commitments. By diverting the conversation from a serious analysis of food ethics, the speaker avoids a thoughtful reexamination of the contents of her or his dinner plate and reinforces the dominant discourse that excludes veg*n voices.

Queerness also threatens patriarchal hierarchies by presenting an alternative to the traditional heterosexual model. As veg*ns struggle to make their meanings understood within a culture fiercely committed to meat-eating, LGBTQQIA people struggle to make their meanings understood within a culture that only accepts the legitimacy of heterosexual relations.

What is of moral, personal, political, and existential importance to veg*ns, LGBTQQIA people, and other marginalized people often becomes entertainment for those who wish to discuss, but not seriously engage with what it means to be veg*n, queer, or otherwise marginalized.

I found this to be very much true to the process of coming out as a vegan and a queer person. While I have found so much acceptance and love among my friend groups and Bay Area communities, only a few members of my family know that I am vegan, and even fewer know that I am queer. I have largely kept silent about my dietary choices and sexuality because I know that my family ascribes to the Western cultural values that hold queer-vegan perspectives to be illegitimate, illogical, and inferior.

When I first told my mom about my sexuality, she advised, "You are just going to have to play up the parts of yourself that you want other people to know about."

Still recovering from the stress of coming out, I just nodded.

Earnestly, she said, "You know that I love you. And I am sure you knew I would be accepting."

"I didn't know what to expect. I just didn't know. And I'm worried about the rest of the family."

"Yes, it's going to be really hard for some of them, like your grandparents, to accept it. It's probably best if we don't tell them for now."

Again, I nodded.

"It'll be okay. This doesn't have to be the focus of your life."

And later, when I told my mom about my veganism, she responded, "I just think you're being really extreme."

"Mom, this is something that I really care about."

"Can't you see my point of view? You're always fighting the way I raised you. I always tried my best to give you what I thought were healthy meals."

"Yes, I know you did, Mom. This isn't some attack on the values you raised me with. Animals are being tortured and killed for me to eat meat and I'm not okay with that."

"Well, this isn't the kind of thing that you can commit to for a lifetime."

Smiling, I responded, "Oh, we'll see about that."

What I find interesting here is the rhetorical similarities in my mom's responses to my queerness and veganism. Because there is no conceptual space to mediate queer and vegan experiences, veganism and queerness are deemed unsustainable, unhealthy, "extreme," unimportant, and something to be hidden from other people.

The Sexual Politics of Meat has shown me that there are cultural dimensions to the disempowerment and silencing of vegan and queer voices. Thus, queer and vegan activism can build a world where all lives are treated with respect and dignity. It has also shown me that this better world is possible. As Adams so beautifully puts it, "There is something on the other side of this culture of oppression—and that something is better, better for us, better for the environment, better for our relationships, better for the animals." In our struggles to build a world free of human and animal oppression, it is essential that, as vegan-feminists, we push ourselves to act in solidarity with struggles against homophobia, ableism, racism, religious discrimination, imperialism, classism, capitalism, and all other manifestations of violence and oppression. It's also important that our allies in this struggle recognize that equality for all is not possible until human-animal relations promote, in the words of Adams, "organic unity rather than disjunction; harvest rather than violence; living in harmony rather than having domain over." After all, as *The Sexual Politics of Meat* shows us, whom we choose to consume either embodies or negates our commitments to feminism and equality.

In college I quickly found my voice in the global Occupy movement. In many ways, the Occupy movement embodies the type of activism that *The Sexual Politics of Meat* dares us to envision, by moving away from single-issue politics and fighting the fragmentation of the struggle for liberation and equality. At my first Occupy protest I proudly carried a sign that read "Corporations Are Making a Killing: Stop Animal and Worker Exploitation." The sign started many conversations with non-animal activists, and I quite liked that.

Sustaining Rice

CAROLYN MULLIN

"*W*hat does your ankle say?"

I get that question at least a few times a week, especially in the summer when my jeans have been swapped out for shorter apparel and my tattoo is more visible.

"Eat rice have faith in women," I say.

I've always liked rice. It's a universal crop that sustains even the poorest of communities, including that of my family in Mexico. In many patriarchal societies where men consume much of the available protein, it is this simplest of carbohydrates that sustains women, who in turn sustain the household, the family. Dietary choices, women's empowerment, and community building go hand-in-hand, connections that Fran Winant, author of the poem "Eat Rice Have Faith in Women," has reflected upon in her verses.

Rice is one of the few dishes I made as a college kid living in a modest dorm at the University of Florida. Black beans and rice with a bit of seasoning was dinner at least once a week. My culinary repertoire has grown and significantly improved in color, quality, and flavor since then, but rice still has its special place: warm yellow dhal over basmati rice, a simple stir-fry with fresh farmers market veggies, teriyaki tofu and brown rice, and Mexican rice with seitan mole enchiladas, a specialty of my mom's, who was born and raised in Mexico City.

I don't look like the stereotypical Mexican-American (what's typical these days, anyhow?). My mother's side of the family refers to me as *la güerita*, little white girl, a Goldilocks with light eyes. These characteristics don't compute with the five-foot-one, dark-skinned woman who birthed me. People told my mother that she was deluding herself in thinking she could have a blond-haired, blue-eyed child; but never underestimate the power of marrying someone with the traits you want in a kid and praying to El Señor.

My Latina heritage, with its color, warmth, and vibrancy, is one that I have embraced and one with which I have struggled as well. Between the childhood friends I made and have kept from my hometown of Miami, Florida, my family members still in Mexico whom I see every once in a while, and the close-knit circle of Latina ladies that I've come to know and love through my work with Casa Dolores, a Mexican folk art museum in Santa Barbara, I consider myself a very lucky woman. There was an almost instantaneous bond forged with these women—camaraderie, understanding, and empathy for one another came about so naturally, effortlessly. I can't say the same for all my interactions with the opposite sex.

It isn't my intention to make grand assumptions or generalizations, but I can speak from my own experiences. I've come to know quite a few considerate and compassionate Latino men over the years, but machismo exists. It is reiterated and fed in many different ways, sometimes by women, and puts women between juxtaposing roles. On the one hand, women are to strive to be in the likeness of La Virgen de Guadalupe—humble, pious, virtuous—and on the other, they are desired for their sensuality and alluring nature, like Mexican calendar girls.

The same mentality can be found wherever you go, but it seems quite ingrained in many Latin cultures. I recently struggled with this while co-curating an exhibit at Casa Dolores. We had decided to do a women's show. "Great! We can feature artistic interpretations of powerful Mexican icons—La Virgen, Adelitas of the Revolution, and Sor Juana," I piped in. But in our collection of over 6,000 objects, we sorely lacked strong female representation. Or so I believed.

What we *could* do was a show on women's roles and crafts—in the kitchen preparing foods, weaving textiles, or fashioning ceramics for sale in the market or for use in the home. Even the *soldaderas*, female soldiers of the Mexican Revolution, had been slaves in the kitchen. Literally, many were slaves, taken away from their families and towns and forced into a life of service. (A few managed to get on the front lines by cloaking themselves in men's apparel, but mostly they were relegated to supporting roles.) I felt defeated. I wanted to depict women doing something besides domestic work, but these are the roles they, Mexico's poor and its artisans, generally have, and that they carry out with strength, integrity, and out of necessity.

Eat rice have faith in women.

Through these arts, which are now sought the world over by collectors and tourists, Mexican artisans have been able to unleash their creativity, indomitable spirit, and enterprising nature while helping to make ends meet. Folk artists use whatever material is available (dirt = pottery, aluminum = an ornament, newspaper = papier-mâché to make their art). They are environmental stewards in this regard, repurposing, recycling, and reusing found objects and mediums. And as more and more men leave Mexico to earn much-needed income in the States, it is the women who are left behind that must keep the family intact, the household running, and some income coming in.

In the end, we had a hybrid of the two visions for the exhibition. Utilizing what was in the collection, we managed to include *brujas* (witches), busty mermaids made by Oaxacan artist Josefina Aguilar, and calendar girls—all fascinating components to the exhibit, but each with their own feminist issues. Here's a sample from the text panel accompanying the calendar girls of the exhibit:

> The image of the traditional Mexican woman was reinvented and modernized to add seductive power to advertising products. These girls were painted to be enticing, alluring, and sometimes racy. While most of the calendar girls represented Mexico through their dress, poses, or props, they were always portrayed as fantasy girls who often appeared to be European or North American. The calendar girls and Mexico's turn-of-the-century archetype of feminine beauty was (and still is) characterized by fair skin, high cheekbones, long legs, and cosmopolitan hairstyles. On the calendars, many of the pinup scenarios included cowgirls and revolutionaries wearing high heels and holding up bottles of beer or tequila, masa-grinding mothers in fashionable jewelry and contemporary hairstyles, bare-chested or naked women in exotic locations, and women dressed in Indian costumes sometimes holding a basket or plastic baby doll. The calendars were produced from 1930 to 1960 and are still thought of fondly and nostalgically.

Feminists can have a field day picking out sections to comment on, as there are so many themes here to explore: Westernization, "sex sells" advertising, romanticizing the foreign and the exotic. It's with the latter that I can relate to. In some interactions with Latino men,

I have felt that I was on view, on exhibition, similar to the afore-mentioned calendar girls. Apparently, I'm this exotic Americanized version of *Mexicanidad* (Mexicanness). As soon as the Spanish words come out of my lips with some semblance of fluency and men learn that I'm half Mexicana, they give me the seal of approval. The compliments start rolling out and these men start asking if I'm already spoken for. And these are the gentlemen that are at least engaging in a conversation. I've heard enough yells of "¡Oye, mami!" from cars passing me by on the streets to last a lifetime.

BEFORE MY WORK with the folk art museum and founding the National Museum of Animals & Society (NMAS), I headed Farm Sanctuary's California Education Department. It was difficult to leave the hundreds of animals, human and nonhuman, whom I befriended during my years at the sanctuary and who put faces, names, and stories to the facts and figures we, as activists, communicate to the public. The residents put into personal context much of what I'd read about: the rape of animals (female pigs and turkeys are "artificially inseminated"), words that mask cruelty (culling vs. killing, beef vs. cow), and much more. If you've never spent much time with farmed animals, make plans to head out to your nearest farm animal sanctuary soon! These animals and their tales of survival are so moving, inspiring, and life-changing. You'll never be the same, and you'll see farm animals as *present referents* for who they are: enchanting, loving, sentient beings.

I had been ruminating on the idea of the museum for some years. I wondered where the old horse ambulances that rescued exhausted or injured workhorses from the early twentieth century had gone, what stories remained from canines on the battlefields of World War

Two, and what artifacts existed from Jack London's humane youth organization and its work to convince Ringling Brothers to stop using animals in the circus.

Farm Sanctuary was an exceptional place with a pioneering vision that had a history of its own to be recorded. Because they allow farmed animals to live out their entire lives, Farm Sanctuary has become an expert in farm animal geriatrics. In just twenty-five years, their model has inspired many individuals to start their own shelters, saving lives and teaching compassion in different parts of the country and the world. This was the galvanizing, innovative, and thoughtful energy of a movement I wanted to see in a museum setting.

When I left the farm and ventured into the museum, I vowed to preserve and share the history of our movement, which as an organized effort dates back to the same era as the birth of abolitionism, women's suffrage, labor struggles, and even children's welfare (give or a take a few decades). Until NMAS, animal protection was the only social justice cause that did not have its own institution preserving, interpreting, and sharing its incredible legacy. I had long had a penchant for museums and collecting, and have had the privilege to work in a number of museums to date: historical, art, science, and children's, too.

NMAS became the first museum of its kind dedicated to "enriching the lives of animals and people through exploration of our shared experience" and focusing on the (living) history of the animal protection movement, human-animal studies, and humane education. A signed copy of *The Sexual Politics of Meat* is already in the museum's library (along with Adams' other works), and I've been petitioning Carol Adams to donate her old carousel slide projector and her original slides to the museum's collection. She laughed for a good long minute when I initially made the suggestion to her. I think she was surprised that someone would want an old, beat-up projector that jams.

I love the projector as an artifact. It not only tells a story of an antiquated technology but, in this case, of an object that forever transformed the animal rights and feminist movements, academic theory, and generations of young women. Design-wise, construction of the carousel speaks to female representation as well, circles being an almost universal symbol of femininity. Feminists for Animal Rights (FAR), on whose board Carol Adams served, has for their logo a fox curled up inside the female or Venus symbol. I love how Carol's story, those of women around the world, and the slideshow come full circle, literally.

Imagine us reliving the original slideshow in fifty or a hundred years for an entirely new audience that probably never will have known this sort of equipment. One can only hope that it'll be a vegan, feminist world by then (this is the inscription on our copy of Adams' book—"Yours for a vegan, feminist world. –Carol"), and those museumgoers will say, "Can you imagine when people still thought and acted like that? How barbaric."

Now that the National Museum of Animals & Society is in full swing as an institution and my brain has been attuned to catch the absent referent at work, I see that the museum field is speckled with examples that provide a fascinating and morally challenging discussion in light of animals and their bodies. Animals remain one of the most popular exhibition themes. The most heavily trafficked type of museum is zoos. (Zoos are technically considered museums, and their collections are the live animals exhibited within their compounds.) Many books have been written on the ethics and welfare of these animals in captivity, but less has been researched on those other museum animals, the dead ones displayed in natural history museums and art museums.

In displaying the preserved corpses of animals, they become an absent referent. One example is Knut the polar bear. The beloved artic mammal who was born at the Berlin Zoo drew the world's gaze (what cute baby mammal and his antics wouldn't?) and became an international sensation.

In 2011, Knut unexpectedly passed away at the tender age of four from encephalitis. Then began the deluge of mourning rituals—press coverage, flowers, memorials, commemorative statue—and questions surrounding the future of his body. Will he be buried? Cremated? In the end, his body was sent to a natural history museum for "preservation." Both the zoo and the museum, despite public outrage, felt his body would do more good in a museum setting, serving as an interpretive object on the issue of global warming and wildlife conservation.

Technically, the taxidermied Knut is a work of art. A taxidermist must build or purchase the "insides"; a century ago this would have meant using wool, wood, wire, and plaster to create a mannequin, while today Styrofoam shapes are readily available. Taxidermists have the power to stage an animal's position and facial expressions. Tigers, for instance, are infamous for their carnivorous teeth, which are flaunted in natural history institutions and no doubt generate shock and awe. Doing so fortifies the idea of a predator. But we also know that tigers have a softer side, especially in terms of rearing their young. In taxidermy, I see the absent referent at play. A body detached from his bearhood. A body devoid of personality. A body used for another purpose altogether, and without consent. A consumable entity for the masses. Couldn't a statue serve the same purpose and achieve the same results, minus the ethical quandaries?

Even if the zoo and museum decided to forgo displaying Knut, they would have preserved his body as a specimen, for future use in scientific research. Bodies of whales washed ashore, dolphins, giant squid, and other animals become highly sought after by museum and research institutions. What does that signify in terms of our respect or reverence for life? For animals? For our own humanity?

In the art world, there's a whole new chapter of animal use to consider. Artists have starved dogs as a theme (e.g., Guillermo Vargas Jiménez's *Exposición No. 1* at Galeria Codice in Managua, Nicaragua) and attempted to have live chickens displayed in a museum with a slaughter and communal meal to follow (United Poultry Concerns helped to halt Amber Hansen's *The Story of Chickens: A Revolution* at the Spencer Museum in Kansas). The Berlin anatomist-artist Gunther von Hagens uses plastination to preserve bodies and argues that his latest show, *Animal Inside Out* (at the Natural History Museum in London, England), will inspire budding biologists with its exposure of blood vessels and leg muscles in a stop-animation sort of taxidermy. The source of some of these bodies has not been made public.

I get asked often whether or not NMAS, when we open our building, will have animals, alive or dead, on exhibit. There is certainly tremendous power in connecting with a living being: someone, not something. I witnessed that firsthand at Farm Sanctuary. People can be transformed by the connection; so much that they'll change their habits, dietary choices and overall lifestyle in order to safeguard animals. At NMAS, we are cognizant of the absent referent and use it as a litmus test when contemplating future exhibitions, programming, and outreach efforts.

SOME MONTHS AGO Carol Adams was presenting her slide-show in Santa Barbara, California; a version that had been updated since the one I had hosted during my collegiate years. The most rewarding and challenging part of her lecture was seeing young faces in the audience ask the same questions I and my peers had posed nearly a decade ago. It reaffirmed my growing belief that our work as activists is and most likely will never be done; with each new generation the most basic of principles—equality, humanity, compassion—must be instilled and fostered over and over again. It's a painful lesson, for us and other animals, and a daunting challenge that I don't think animal advocates and all social justice activists have quite come to terms with. We don't want to believe that we have to start from scratch on a regular basis, but we do.

One example of this is the fur-free campaign. In the 1980s, over 8,000 people could be seen at a New York City Fur-Free Friday march to protest the cruelties of the fur industry and to encourage stores, on their busiest shopping day of the year, to stop selling fur. Awareness spread, stores pulled fur from their racks, and the demand for pelts fell dramatically. It was no longer popular to wear fur. Claiming victory and pressing forward onto other issues, activists didn't feel the need to educate the next generation about fur, didn't keep on top of the industry with public pressure, resulting in fur now being back in fashion. That was a painful lesson for activists and even more painful for fur-bearing animals who were killed for their pelts.

Through NMAS, we are showing that people have been speaking up for animals for centuries. And we demonstrate that animal abuse issues (farmed animal welfare, vivisection, and others), have been dealt with time and time again. Should it really take centuries to get the hint and bring about lasting change?

Today's school-age children are educated about women's suffrage, civil rights, and other important movements either through lesson plans, days of remembrance, or celebratory months (Women's History Month, Black History Month, César Chavez Day). To recognize the animal protection movement in this way would foster generation after generation of socially aware global citizens. This is a goal and a priority of the museum.

Carol certainly is doing her part to engage both young and old to think critically about their values, attitudes, and assumptions, and is keeping up her educational efforts for young people. Through NMAS's exhibitions, collection, and humane education programs, we're striving to do the same. And we'll be sure to keep Carol's legacy and her revolutionary work on the sexual politics of meat alive. She deserves it and I surmise future generations will still need it.

Eat rice have faith in women.

There is an empty space on my ankle. The words encircle it, but not all the way around. That was intentional. I've come a long way as a person and an activist since I was at the tattoo parlor, but my journey is far from over. I'm hoping to live to a hundred, which gives me another seventy-one years to bring about positive change: change in the way other animals are viewed and treated, how society understands and perceives the animal protection movement, and how people understand and improve their many relationships with other animals. I want to fill that empty spot with something representative of the work I do in this next part of my life, which I'm sure will continue to be inspired by Carol and her life's work.

Dog

Knowing Ignorance

VIDUSHI SHARMA

$\mathcal{V}$egetarian.

Until I was twelve years old, I thought the word was just something multisyllabic and unnecessary. It was what I'd hear my parents say to servers at restaurants, or see my teachers check off on school field trip forms. I learned to say it with the same precision as they did, conveying the *V* with a swift push of breath through the lips and an offhand pride. It was a strange word, prompting both smiles and slight recoils, distant bewilderment. But it was as much a part of me as my dark eyes and hair, and I didn't realize it needed an explanation.

I grew up in a full-blooded Indian family of Hindus and Buddhists. Hindi was my first language; my mother would tack a little sheet of translations onto my backpack after we moved to America so that my preschool teachers could understand me. My summers were Indian summers: full of secret adventures with my cousins around my grandparents' lemon tree grove in Lucknow, playing tricks on the local guards, and befriending street dogs, the source of parental paranoia. Humid, rainy, rich, and always colorful. My north

Indian relatives came from all backgrounds; I spent my time around everyone, from Sanskrit teachers to professors of engineering, from astrophysicists to rural farmers. We spanned a spectrum of colors— although there were variations in skin tone from light to darker, I was fascinated by the differences in our eyes. Some, like mine, were so dark that the irises seemed indistinguishable from the pupils, while others' were pale gray or hazel. Among differences of professions, skin, and eyes, vegetarianism was a binding cultural glue.

It just made sense. Vegetarianism accompanied traditional Hindu-Buddhist philosophical values on life and nonviolence— known as ahimsa. Human actions had karmic consequences; by inflicting pain and suffering upon other beings, we would ensure reciprocity. By ingesting animal bodies, we would concurrently ingest their fear and anguish prior to slaughter, blocking ourselves from a higher consciousness. But I was too young for these ideas to be more than just a background buzz in my mind. All I knew was that, as a quiet child who appreciated wrapping herself in solitude, animals granted me intense and sudden joy.

I found ways to love nature regardless of what continent I was on. I grew up in a small community in New Jersey along the Hackensack River, walking along river trails to feed ducks and watching the sun set almost every day. I pretended the muskrats and groundhogs that sometimes burrowed under my neighbors' garages were my friends. When the town's animal control group put cages around their holes, my best friend and I plastered the site with handmade posters urging kind treatment. (The group sent us a note in reply— they didn't intend to harm the creatures, but just to relocate them.) After reading bird-watching manuals, I soon could easily identify the egrets, herons, ducks, and cormorants that nested and fed along the river. That people might intentionally harm animals didn't occur to me for some time, and combining this with my family background, I never questioned why I was a vegetarian.

As I grew older, I realized that most people didn't see vegetarianism as simply as I did. In elementary school, I often faced classmates who were narrow-minded and skeptical about my leafy sandwiches and Indian bread rolls. Sometimes, I'd come home in tears because of someone's distaste for my food and blurt out to my parents that I *hated* bringing vegetarian lunches to school. *This is your choice,* they'd explain after briefly exchanging glances. *If you want to start eating meat, that's okay.* Slowly I realized that vegetarianism was a conscious choice, not a family heirloom. It wasn't a clunky irrelevant word anymore; it was my lifestyle.

With this knowledge, I became eager to talk about vegetarianism whenever I could. In fifth grade, some of my friends went vegetarian after I said that I didn't eat meat because I was an animal lover. After all, every trendy ten-year-old girl loved animals. We proclaimed it by decorating our binders with stickers of puppies and kittens; I started a movement to bring soft toy monkeys to class, to my fifth-grade teacher's amusement. *How can you love this golden retriever puppy and then eat a cow?* I'd ask. My logic clicked with a few friends, but I wasn't always received so well, especially over the lunch table in a stifling cafeteria. The day I asked my best friend why she was eating parts of dead animals, she didn't talk to me for the rest of the hour. I deserved it—I hadn't phrased it in the wisest way. In my desperate and slightly angry way of explaining vegetarianism, I only managed to alienate her.

It was confusing for me as a young girl to think that my favorite teachers, friends, and relatives made daily conscious choices to eat meat. When I heard older mentors using the same evasive arguments about meat that my fifth-grade friends did, I was crushed. I could understand why a classmate might put forth a case like, "If we didn't eat meat, cows would overpopulate the planet" or "Meat just tastes too good," but a teacher? An older relative?

The first real sense of betrayal I felt was after watching a slaughterhouse video when I was thirteen. It was a dim Saturday evening, and family friends were visiting for dinner. My mother and father were bustling around, transporting steaming spiced dishes with their distinct laughter from kitchen to dining room. I had escaped upstairs, aimlessly clicking around on websites on our old desktop computer, when I arrived at a vegetarian documentary website. My eyes locked onto a video that I *knew* I shouldn't be watching. It was labelled in bright red type, made by undercover reporters in a factory farm. I ignored the apprehension running through my mind and clicked.

A slow, cold numbness curled through my body. Distressed cows thrashed around in execution and their eventual carcasses flitted across the screen. A loud jumble of workers' voices accompanied the violent tossing of chickens into boiling vats; one worker jumped upon a young pig's body. It was a terrible feeling. I couldn't bear to watch any more—but I was physically unable to stop. After the bloody video ended, I remained in my chair, blankly staring at the screen. I shot up after hearing my mother's footsteps, fumbling to close the website, and then disappeared with a hurried slam into the bathroom. I found myself crying silently. For me, the connection between death and meat consumption would never again be absent. I felt inherently betrayed by every smiling, loving family member, schoolteacher, or friend who had made the consumption of meat from factory farms a willing and regular part of their diet. At the same time, my mind had a hard time labelling the integral people in my life as cruel.

A simple fact was made clear to me that evening: not all adults were perfect, even the ones I loved. I started drawing myself inward and stopped explaining my moral choices to anyone. Some people were hostile to the idea of vegetarianism, and I was similarly bitter toward them. With quiet stubbornness, I twisted away from uncomfortable questions regarding my vegetarianism.

I gradually adopted an offhand casual pride in attributing my vegetarian lifestyle to environmental reasons. After all, hard numbers are difficult to dispute, and most people didn't even try. Who would argue with the amount of carbon dioxide released into the air per pound of meat, the inefficiency of beef production, or deforestation per half-pound of hamburger? Trying to reach out to my classmates, I presented the environmental impacts of meat eating to my eighth-grade English class. I later revised and expanded this speech for a Latin oratory class as a sophomore in high school. I was well-received, but failed in making any real connection with my classmates by streamlining my focus on the problems with meat eating to what might be most convenient for them to think about.

Never did I mention my ethical issues with meat eating, although I internally squirmed in the oratory class when I heard a presentation calling for the end to the abuse of dolphins coming from someone who ate meat. Similarly, when one meat-loving classmate brought up her "love" for animals and horrified reaction to abuse in a discussion about hunting in my English class, I couldn't help but feel conflicted. No one seemed to be making the link between human and animal abuse and meat consumption.

Then, a few months ago, my cell phone buzzed late at night, signaling a text message. I was awake reading a book, and fumbled around before flipping my phone open. "So," it read, "I'm a vegetarian now . . ."

The sender of the message was a close friend of mine who had ribbed me for my own vegetarianism for almost as long as I'd known him. He had often joked about starting a Meat Club in response to my dedication to the Vegetarian Club at school, casually dropping references to my alleged "moral superiority complex" or to his own love of meat or *Epic Meal Time*, a bacon-and-whiskey-heavy cooking show. These responses probably weren't meant to be serious; I mentally grouped them with the other immature remarks my classmates made about vegetarianism. His news should have surprised me, but instead I mostly felt a warm sense of acknowledgment. I already felt familiar with my friend's decision because on the inside, I needed to.

I needed to realize that others felt and thought as I did, that I wasn't alone. After years of distancing myself from others about vegetarianism and the other deeper parts of my life, I wanted to relate to someone outside my family circle. As two students interested in philosophy, my friend and I often discussed moral issues or readings for hours. He gave me a copy of Descartes' *Meditations on First Philosophy* and I showed him the Bhagavad Gita. But through all this, I never broached the topic of vegetarianism. I valued his friendship the same after he became vegetarian as I had before, but my outlook toward talking to other people about ethical issues changed. I felt comfortable trusting others and speaking to them honestly and openly about ideas as personal as my vegetarianism.

A few weeks ago I was visiting a Green Festival in my hometown and came across a lady campaigning for the humane treatment of dogs in shelters and the end of puppy mills. Her tent attracted many sympathetic visitors, young and old. Her mission was heartening, but I couldn't help wondering whether the woman herself was aware of the widespread animal abuse in factory farms. I couldn't bring myself to ask, and maneuvered around her table to speak with other vendors and grassroots organizations, even walking along the marshy boardwalk for some time to watch the kayaks. But after thinking about how long I had resisted talking about vegetarianism to other people and possibly losing the chance to open them to new ideas, I decided to approach her.

We had a predictable conversation at first, and she gave me information about problems with puppy mills and pet breeders. Before leaving, I asked the woman if she was, by chance, vegetarian. A quick expression of surprise flitted across her face, and she assured me that some others in her organization were vegetarian. I asked if she was aware of the treatment of animals on factory farms. She nodded sympathetically, though she admitted she wasn't very knowledgeable, and listened to me talk about how animal rights was wider in scope than many realized. We amenably talked about the meat industry a little bit before I left. I may or may not have prompted her to think more about meat consumption as related to animal activism. Though she seemed receptive and agreed with me about factory farming being unethical, it was clear that she had never deeply thought about the issues of her food. Then, I had to think— did anyone truly always face uncomfortable issues head-on?

I realized with a slight shock, *I didn't*. There were universally oppressed groups that I imagined as free, of which I continued to support the oppression. Take battery hens, for example. I am aware of the ethical issues surrounding mass-consumed, factory-farmed eggs, but still am not vegan. I try my best to find eggs and milk from responsible sources, but my tennis shoes, car seats, and home furniture are still leather. I utilize the possible products of sweatshops or unfair labor plants—the MacBook I'm typing on, for example. Where is the boundary that separates the normal from the cruel?

Today, I am still not sweatshop- or cruelty-free. My parents are uncomfortable with veganism for the same reason that many people are uncomfortable with vegetarianism—concerns about nutrition. But as a vegetarian tennis player, I've never faced problems with fitness because of my parents' laserlike attention to our family diet. Deep red beet-carrot-apple juices are a regular weekend brew, spinach and egg whites a normal part of almost every breakfast. My father takes quiet pride in his small indoor crop of wheatgrass, extracting juice that the whole family drinks every morning. Our daily Indian lentil dishes are naturally protein-rich, and homemade yogurt and smoothies are a constant part of most of our meals. However, right now, veganism is incompatible with my parents' food lifestyles, so I have to be content with the least harmful-sounding organic milk products and local eggs I can find.

It's frustrating to question whether the girl I have seen myself as for years—ethically conscious, respectful of all life—might just be a specter of my imagination. When I was younger, I coined the term "knowing ignorance" for myself as an expression for when people deliberately avoided exposing themselves to information about issues for fear of discomfiting themselves. The absent referent that Carol Adams talks about in *The Sexual Politics of Meat*, which disconnects the meat eater from the animal and the animal from a meal, is an example of "knowing ignorance." So is Jonathan Safran Foer's definition of cruelty in *Eating Animals* as "not only the willful causing of unnecessary suffering, but the indifference to it." I know about the dairy industry and still enjoy milk chocolate. I've seen videos of cruelty to hens and still enjoy egg-sourced cakes. Have I been the knowingly ignorant one all along?

Right now, I'm not sure.

I was taking the F subway train in New York uptown one day this summer, seated in a crowded car and discreetly reading *The Sexual Politics of Meat*, with the book on top of my backpack. I was aware that a plump and cheery-looking lady had looked over to see what I was reading, and I paid her no attention. But suddenly, I felt her shift slightly and say, "Excuse me. That book you're reading . . ."

I love random interactions with people, especially in places as diverse as New York City.

"Yes." I smiled and nodded, hoping she'd go on.

"I just found the title really interesting," she said, "because my yoga teacher mentioned something similar the other day. He warns people against feeding their children meat before the age of three, because it awakens sexual desires in one of their chakras."

At this point, I looked across from me and saw a group of people listening to our conversation and looking slightly troubled. I hadn't known before that some people connected meat-eating to sexual tendencies, but I wanted to keep speaking with the woman. I explained what the main point of the book was—connecting the socially ignored oppression of animals to the oppression of women—and asked if she was vegetarian. She laughed embarrassedly, her curly afro bobbing a little. "No, not yet," she said. "But I try to source my meat responsibly. There's a farm in Queens that lets you choose your cow for slaughter for something around $300, and a halal meat place in the city in a warehouse that does something similar."

Of course I'm against eating meat on any level, for ethical reasons. But it is more acceptable to me when people are aware of the problems with factory-farmed meat and make an attempt to eat flesh that has been naturally raised and killed with less suffering. I asked what had motivated her to become a more conscious consumer. "I just had a baby," she responded. "I'm feeling like my choices affect more than just me now."

Maybe that's it. The Bhagavad Gita, a tenet of Indian philosophy, insists that all souls are not only connected but essentially one.

When people start realizing the web of links weaving their lives together with those of other humans and other animals, a more compassionate lifestyle will seem natural. Sometimes, the simplest ethical cases make the most sense to people. For a long time, in an effort to reach more people, I confined myself to clear-cut arguments about health, climate change, and pollution. But by catering to the preconceived notions of my peers and pointing out the problems meat-eating causes and not the problems *with* meat-eating, a distinction that Carol Adams also draws, I may have been adding to the very culture of willing ignorance that I despise. My close friend made the switch because of reaching one unembellished ethical conclusion: eating meat is morally wrong because it causes unnecessary suffering. From a utilitarian standpoint, he didn't value the enjoyment he got from eating an animal's flesh over the suffering that animal experienced.

Growing up as a vegetarian, I've been in a lot of discussions that have ended negatively. I've been disillusioned by many friends and mentors and upset by people's knowing ignorance, more so than even by the facts that I continue to learn about the damage caused by the meat industry. But after it all, I've become a more open seventeen-year-old who is less likely to underestimate people's capacity to think about personal moral issues. I went through a time of negativity toward meat eaters in my life whom I thought of as hypocritical, but have learned to see people through a wider perspective. Vegetarianism is just one issue in life; it's both unfair and counterproductive for me to make judgments about character based upon it. My vegetarianism is intrinsically connected to the philosophy I have grown up with and my outlook on life and people. Now, it is something that I embrace discussing, both to advocate for ethically conscious consumption and to continue to unearth more about myself and the world I'm in.

Beyond Band-Aid Work

ASHLEY MAIER

$\mathcal{I}$ began my career in a very large Midwestern hospital as an advocate for women who were experiencing domestic violence. I had known since graduate school that I wanted to work on big-picture change—I wanted to create systems change/social change to keep problems from occurring in the first place. After yet another week of crisis work that included taping an emergency cell phone onto a woman's body under her clothing, fighting to help several abused women keep their children, and arguing with a doctor that he couldn't refuse to discharge a woman from the hospital because her husband was violent toward her, I was fed up. A colleague and I guiltily confessed to each other that we believed we were doing "Band-Aid work." We were tired of waiting for women to experience abuse and then come to us—as if women should expect this from men. We wanted to do *prevention*, but all anyone seemed to be doing was going and talking to high school students about creating good boundaries so they could avoid abuse. There had to be something more: something that struck at the root.

During that time, I received a pamphlet from Vegan Outreach. I had been vegetarian for almost a decade, but I had never known the realities behind dairy and egg production. The pamphlet woke me up. It wasn't long before I was comparing the same entitlement, power, and control core in domestic violence to what I saw was happening in factory farms. Pamphlet in hand, I flashed back to a few weeks earlier, when I was sitting in a hospital room with a woman who was in intensive care after having been stabbed by her boyfriend. With her chest tube draining by my feet, she told me about how her boyfriend wouldn't let her go to school or work, tracked the miles on the car to make sure she only went where he told her to, and never let her see her friends and family. It escalated one night when he found out that her mother called while he was out of the apartment. He accused her of all sorts of horrible things, she said, and attacked.

Thinking about the visit, I wasn't struck by his clear desire to control every aspect of her life—I heard those stories every day. That's domestic violence. What stood out in my mind is what she said to me next. Staring ahead, appearing numb, she told me there is nothing worse than having choices taken away from you. When I asked her how I could help, what she wanted, she said she didn't know, she just wanted it to be on her own terms. She wanted to live her life. Thinking about this woman who just wanted to make her own decisions, I began to educate myself more about the ways in which factory farming takes choices away. I became a strict vegan, and then, well, the shit hit the fan.

I think anyone who has discovered something new or made an exciting change wants to discuss it. I sure did. I saw that the movement to end violence against women wouldn't ever succeed if it continued to be in isolation from other movements. *Look what else is out there, creating a culture that allows this power-over mentality and violence to continue!* I'd say. And then I learned to shut my mouth if I wanted to keep my job and stay in the movement.

I'll never forget the day when, standing by the fax machine and talking about my recent conversion to veganism, a colleague I looked up to very much as a social justice superstar told me veganism was too extreme. I was shocked. Any enthusiasm for the conversation drained right out of me. If someone who so acutely understood oppression and so effectively advocated for other social justice issues thought veganism was extreme, was there any hope? And it wasn't just her. Several other colleagues told me I was going too far. They lamented the fact that there were so many animal shelters and so few women's shelters. The very same dichotomous "either/or" thinking that I learned to reject as a feminist ruled the movement that had been my home. *It's us or the animals.*

I couldn't believe it. People, friends, and mentors who were so strongly against oppression, who I really felt "got it," didn't get this. My choice was to be ostracized or to shut up. I shut up. I left my job and moved to Southern California.

In Southern California, I immediately connected with a local animal rights organization. I told the founder, a fellow feminist, of my frustrations and she suggested I look into the work of Carol Adams. She also put me in touch with another woman who had worked in the field of sexual violence and who had expressed similar sentiments and experiences. We had both been feeling utterly alone, rejected within the movement to end violence against women, and desperate. I bought a copy of *The Sexual Politics of Meat*, met with the woman (who would become a lifelong friend and ally in this work), got a violence-prevention job, and never looked back.

What I found in *The Sexual Politics of Meat* was a treasure. It was like a trusted friend who showed me I wasn't alone. A gift that I couldn't *believe* had been kept from me for so long. Why was no one in my movement talking about this? Why did I have such a horrible

time getting vegan meals at domestic violence-prevention conferences? Why did I feel I had to hide my veganism from fellow feminists and violence-prevention advocates, and why did they ridicule
me when they discovered I was vegan? It was all right there, in an
amazing book written fifteen years earlier! Someone had been talking about this for years and yet everyone was still trying to silence
me. My veganism and my feminism, the book confirmed, really did
go hand in hand.

Since I connected with Stacia Mesleh, the woman from the sexual-violence-prevention movement, I wondered if there were others
like her out there. I started talking to more people. I found that it
was safer to talk about *The Sexual Politics of Meat* in a theoretical
setting than in real life, with practitioners and activists. For the most
part, academics would listen, or even agree. Practitioners and activists shut me down. *How impractical*, they would say. This is about
women, not animals. *How insulting*.

Even activists who were willing to talk about the connections
with me did so in hushed whispers. At an anti-oppression weekend
training in Santa Barbara, I was thrilled beyond belief to find another
vegan feminist participating. When it came time for an activity in
which participants split into groups based on social justice issues of
interest, I proposed a group exploring the connections between violence against humans, animals, and the environment. After all, I knew
there was at least one person who would join the group. Wrong. My
fellow vegan feminist came up close to my ear, said in hushed tones
that she would love to join such a group, but she just didn't think it
was "something we can talk about yet." I ended up joining her group
about violence against women—women only.

I'm not going to lie. I'm no academic. When I learn something,
I want to use it. And that's exactly what I did with *The Sexual Poli-*

tics of Meat. Fortunately for me, as I was reading, primary prevention began to catch fire in the movement opposing violence against
women. "Primary prevention," a public health term, refers to efforts
to stop or eliminate a problem before it occurs. A common adage
refers to going to the head of the river to see why bodies are falling in
rather than pulling them out one by one. This involves creating cultural change, building environments that nurture peace and justice,
and replacing negative norms (often unspoken standards for behavior) with positive norms. *The Sexual Politics of Meat* highlighted
exactly where we needed to focus our primary prevention efforts,
and I wanted people to listen.

Back when I was working as an advocate, a woman asked me
if I had any companion animals. I cheerfully told her about my two
rescue pugs, the loves of my life. Tearfully, she responded with the
story of how her husband had killed her beloved pug just a few weeks
ago. He knew that the animal was her only source of love and comfort, and killed her to hurt his wife. Now choking back my own tears,
I told her about how that is an all-too-common tactic that abusers use
to control and hurt people. Groups like the Humane Society were
just starting to bring the connection between pet abuse and domestic
violence to light. Women's shelters were exploring ways to keep cli-
ents' pets safe, too. The woman's story left an indelible mark on me.
When I went to San Diego, I became involved with a group working
to raise awareness about the link. But I still wanted to go deeper.
What about the "hidden" abuse of animals that we see on our plates,
on our clothing, every day? I wanted to add that to the discussion.
But how would that happen when even discussing pet abuse in a
space dedicated to the elimination of violence against women was
still new and located at the margins?

Conferences continued serving chicken breasts and roast beef.

And I found only five or six more people working within the movement who thought about animals at all. When I attended the 2007 National Organization for Women (NOW) conference, there was only one other attendee who asked for "non-violent" food. No one else seemed to connect the dots—except for Elizabeth Farians, cofounder of Feminists for Animal Rights. Honored for a lifetime of feminist work, Farians took the stage one night to accept her award. With audience members shifting in their seats and whispering loudly, she urged us to consider the plight of animals. Was it true? Had I really heard a famous feminist bring up animal rights?! Indeed she had, and I approached her afterward to thank her. She talked to me about the organization Feminists for Animal Rights. The only dampers that evening were the comments that I heard on my way out of that ballroom. *Elizabeth Farians has gone too far. She's getting old and couldn't stop herself from rambling about something that had nothing to do with feminism. This is a conference about women, after all.*

And what was discussed at those conferences about women? On one occasion, Stacia was at a conference that focused on victims of stalking. A woman introducing one of the speakers stated how "cool" the speaker was because each week she wore a different color leather jacket. During the conference many incidents of horrific violence were relayed to a saddened audience, yet the audience laughed and appreciated clothing that had been obtained by violence.

In the late 2000s, primary prevention's popularity increased and my employment continued to focus more and more exclusively on the primary prevention of violence against women. On prevention forums I eased *The Sexual Politics of Meat* into my discussions. *Norms that promote a power-over mentality? Have you ever heard of feminized proteins? Lack of bodily autonomy? Do you know how milk is produced?* I made meager headway, but headway nonetheless. I became an "out" vegan within the movement. I knew the ridicule and fear wouldn't go away, but I had Carol Adams' book backing me up.

Stacia and I wanted to do something more. We had met a few fellow "connectionists," as we came to call ourselves over the years, but we were sure there were more out there. Who else was reading *The Sexual Politics of Meat?* Who else felt like they couldn't talk about their veganism at work? We started Connect the Dots (connect thedotsmovement.com), a project aimed at promoting and building capacity to address the connections between human, animal, and environmental well-being. We now support a growing community of people who connect the dots—something neither one of us previously thought possible.

I believe that most human-focused social justice movements, especially the movement to end violence against women, maintain hierarchies of power. It's humans *over* animals. As long as this mentality persists, justice is beyond our reach. That very same mentality—namely, that me and those like me are better and more important than "others"—so clearly lies at the root of the violence and oppression plaguing our communities. Yet because it threatens our own comfort and our own power, we ignore the violence in aspects of our lives, including what's on our plates. *The Sexual Politics of Meat* doesn't allow for this.

In my specific line of work, I've found Carol Adams' concept of *feminized proteins* to be the most effective means of communicating the relationship. People may not be able to wrap their heads around the idea of an absent referent, but it's hard to deny our reliance on the exploitation of the female reproductive systems for products like eggs and dairy. Moreover, with the new focus on engaging men in the prevention of violence against women, *The Sexual Politics of Meat* provides an indispensible analysis of how meat is tied to traditional notions of masculinity. To engage men, one must commit to a critical analysis of traditional masculinity. As more practitioners accept this strategy, the sexual politics of meat will be all the more relevant.

A couple of years ago, I met with a major player in the movement to engage men in ending violence against women at a national conference. During dinner at a vegan restaurant in L.A., we discussed his vegetarianism and my veganism. I saw his eyes light up when I decided it was safe to take the plunge and discuss my connectionist philosophy with him. We discussed rape culture, lack of bodily autonomy, and similar issues common to our movement and linked them to the treatment of dairy cows, egg-laying hens, and other animals used by humans. After years of rejection by colleagues, I was finally sitting across from one who was engaged, even *excited*, to have the conversation. Imagine how I felt when he called me, after we had both returned back to work on opposite sides of the country, and wanted to continue our conversation. Progress!

For seven years I have been trying to present an expanded view of rape culture at conferences about violence against women. After years of hearing "This is beyond the scope of this conference," in 2012 the Washington Coalition of Sexual Assault Programs was the first to accept my presentation. On May 16, 2012, I presented Expanding Our Lens: The Rape Culture We Don't Discuss to an audience full of sexual-violence-prevention advocates. You can bet the *The Sexual Politics of Meat* was front and center.

When *The Sexual Politics of Meat* was published over twenty years ago, it was considered controversial. From a practical, applied perspective, it still is. I always thought it would be interesting to have a Sexual Politics of Meat: From Theory to Practice training. Slowly but surely, we're on our way there.

My Feminist Continuum

MELINDA FOX

A continuum is described as a continuous sequence in which adjacent elements are not perceptibly different from each other, although the extremes are quite distinct. For me, it encapsulates perfectly how *The Sexual Politics of Meat* has influenced my daily life and truly served as a gateway into my feminism.

My feminist continuum started when I cofounded a student and community animal advocacy group at the University of Florida in 2001. It remains active today and is the longest-running animal protection group among all land-grant institutions in the country. It was nothing short of a coup when we secured university funding to host Carol Adams to present her slideshow on campus. At the time, it was a very big deal that her slideshow was being shown at such an agrocentric university. While it remains one of the most important events of my early campus activism, what came about quietly on the sidelines made the biggest impression of all. I skipped most of my classes to host Carol for the days she was in town. She was interested in hearing from students, visiting Wild Iris, the last feminist bookstore in the state of Florida, and of course spending time with the host student group. She was more than generous all around. Certainly, my fellow group members and those close to me knew what this meant to me personally, but I tried to play it cool (or at least I thought so). I never bared my soul to her about what a "fan" I was of her work, or shared just how much *The Sexual Politics of Meat* had cracked my world open—even to the point that I had gotten words from the text tattooed on my body. I didn't want to freak her out! Plus, I was kind of nervous and felt self-conscious that I wasn't quite as evolved in my feminism.

I was honored to provide an introduction for Carol to the student body at the slideshow event, which was packed with my fellow classmates from the College of Agriculture—some of whom came to give it an open consideration, but many who were ready to take "aim" at what she was presenting and challenge her head-on. I remember wearing heels to the event and being secretly disappointed in myself when Carol showed a slide pointing out that when a woman wears high heels, it creates an illusion of dainty hooves. I was mortified that I was objectifying myself smack dab in the middle of an auditorium full of skeptics and my fellow activists, and most importantly in front of Carol! I tucked my feet deep under my chair. Like most people in the room, I came away from the slideshow contemplating the ways in which women and nonhuman animals are similarly objectified within pop culture, and especially in advertisements. Clearly, I was just starting out on my own personal continuum.

The real defining moment came the next day after Carol said her good-byes and thanked the students and community for hosting her visit. I was determined to spend every second with her and insisted on bringing her to the local rural airport and wait with her until she boarded her plane. As we sat in the waiting room, Carol did something no one had ever done before—she turned to me and asked, "How have you come into your feminism and what has it felt like for you?"

No one had ever asked me about my experience thus far or engaged with me one-on-one about what feminism meant to me. I shocked myself when, for the first time out loud, I shared that my mother had abandoned me and my three older brothers when I was just five years old. I told her how the news spread like wildfire in my neighborhood and how it stigmatized my siblings and me. I told her that I never really identified as a "feminist" growing up because I associated feminism with what incited my mother to leave my family, almost like it was a selfish condition she suffered from, and I felt that what she sought to be liberated from was her own children. For those reasons I pushed it away, unknowingly burying my own liberation and worthiness of equality because of it. It wasn't until much later that I became more open to what feminism meant and recognized I had a distorted concept of what it was.

I went on to share with Carol that becoming an animal rights activist had brought a whole new way of thinking and a new level of compassion to my feminism. Saying this out loud, in the safe space of our conversation with someone as special as Carol, I felt the sense of a great release—and that I was being heard. Carol said that it wasn't uncommon for women to recognize the subjugation of animals before they can identify ways in which they have themselves been subjugated. And in that moment, I knew exactly what she meant. My continuum now had momentum.

The way in which my feminism has continued to stretch and grow from that time has been an interesting journey.

I went on to work for national animal protection organizations as a fundraiser. Certainly, it never occurred to me that I would become someone who raised money for animal advocacy, but because I was passionate about the issues, understood our mission and tactics, and believed we needed a substantial coffer of resources to be effective, I took to it very naturally. What was interesting for me was that it became another manifestation of my feminism, as the majority of donors I worked with directly were women, in fact almost 90 percent. Additionally, the majority of the workforce at these national nonprofits was female, resembling the landscape of grassroots activists, which is mostly made up of girls and women. It was transformative to come to know women on all of these levels. The lesson Carol articulated so clearly to me at the airport that day became a unifying thread throughout all of my professional activism and animal advocacy fund-raising experiences. Women I worked with seemed to recognize their own subjugation by connecting with animals and by acknowledging their suffering and exploitation, confirming the heart of Adams' work where she draws the parallel between speciesism and sexism. Like me, they were all on their own continuum.

Working professionally for an international animal protection organization uncovered more ways of animal exploitation and its connection to deviant, patriarchal power structures than I ever could have imagined—and truthfully, wish I never came to know. The organization was so large and the work was so comprehensive that I struggled to keep up with the sheer breadth of it. I forced myself to keep up with internal communication across teams, the hundreds of press releases and daily media hits. Just when I thought I had heard of everything, a new form of exploitation would emerge or be revealed. These ranged from undercover investigations of abuse at factory farms of male workers sexually abusing pigs and cows, to seizures of "crush videos" where men paid to witness women stomping on baby ducklings and bunnies with stiletto heels, to cases of domestic abuse that escalated to murder when women's abusers used their beloved pets as a way to control them. I came to understand the correlations and interconnections to patriarchal power structures and the exploitation of women and animals.

One day, I was printing out a stack of media clips to study on a plane while I was traveling for work. This was one exercise I did to ensure I kept aware of what the organization was working on. The printer ran out of paper. As I refilled the machine, I picked up the stack from where the printing cycle had left off. I began to read it while waiting for the rest to print. The story on top was about an eight-month-old female Labrador named Sammy who had been seized from an underground sodomy ring where men in their twenties met in the woods to drink, consume porn, and sodomize female dogs. As it turns out, Sammy got loose one night and was hit by a car and suffered a broken leg. She managed to make her way back to her "owner's" house and was in such bad shape she was taken to a local vet. The vet determined that the leg injury may have been what brought her in, but had also discovered that she had serious internal injuries, severe bruising on her backside and anus, and that her tail had been severely dislocated. The vet had the fortitude to alert the local sheriff's department, which then conducted a full-fledged sting operation to break up the deviant "ring." Heartbreakingly, Sammy's injuries were beyond repair and she was euthanized.

I had never heard of such a terrifying activity. I was struck by the fact that these young men worked and lived in areas right next door to women and young girls, and that maybe they even had girlfriends. What also struck me was that this young dog had been treated so maliciously and yet, despite being injured, her innate sense of loyalty brought her right back to her abuser's lair. It literally took my breath away and I dropped to my knees right there in the office. I vowed to myself that I would continue to work both personally and professionally against animal cruelty in whatever manifestation it may take, so that Sammy and billions of other animals wouldn't suffer in vain.

It's almost too much for me to bear witness and contemplate such atrocities, many of which are truly incomprehensible. Like many activists, it's important for me to acknowledge my emotions and practice self-care to avoid succumbing to a level of misanthropy. But knowing how to ride the wave of my own feminist continuum in ways that will continue to raise my consciousness, inspire my activism, and encourage my compassion will help me stay in it for the long haul.

As I write, there are so many happenings in the world that force me to deconstruct exploitations and institutionalized sexism every day. And as I continue to learn about them, it's now instinctual for me to widen my lens (or in some cases, narrow my focus) and acknowledge the intersectionality of these massive critical issues. To me, it's now second nature to identify the connections in a way that is more holistic rather than focusing on one single social justice issue. *The Sexual Politics of Meat* has shown me how to do this. It's a catalyst for my veganism, it's provided a context for why I consume differently, and it continues to be a lens that informs my continued explorations of feminism. It has shaped my ideology and presently shapes my ways of observing and relating to other rights issues and exploitations—and the connections are everywhere.

Disordered Pronouns, Disordered Eating

LAURA WRIGHT

I have to situate myself: I am a middle-class white woman from North Carolina, a state that on May 8, 2012, became the thirty-first to pass an amendment making same-sex marriage constitutionally illegal. According to a *New York Times* article about North Carolina that appeared three days after the passage of Amendment One—the ambiguous and broad text of which reads that *marriage between one man and one woman is the only domestic legal union that shall be valid or recognized in this State*—"Social and religious conservatism and economic populism have historically gone hand-in-hand in a state that, for many decades, consisted largely of small farms and mill towns. Thus in a state that became known for first-rate universities, it was illegal to buy a cocktail for most of the 20th century."

In other words, I exist—and have existed for the majority of my life—in a state (literal, and in many ways figurative) of problematic socially ascribed contradictions, a place that, despite its many forward-thinking actions, enacts codified and tacit rules that disenfranchise members of its populace. I have lived elsewhere—in Massachusetts and New York—and I could argue, I suppose, that things were clearer and less muddled there. But I've come back to North Carolina, and it is from within that literal state and its engagement with these various states of being that I continually seek to enact a vegan feminist social activism informed by Carol Adams' *The Sexual Politics of Meat*, a text I happened upon quite by accident in 2001.

But first things first.

1. I have an early memory of asking my mother why "he" was the universal pronoun. I didn't use the phrase "universal pronoun," but I was conscious at about age five of the fact that "he" was used to mean male or female. Things have changed since then; I am neither young nor exceptionally old, but old enough to remember being a child prior to "they" entering the mainstream lexicon as both singular and gender neutral; at one point, we were all "he."

2. When I was thirteen, my class took a field trip to a fellow classmate's father's sausage processing plant. I never ate sausage again.

3. At the age of nineteen, I stopped eating just about everything.

4. A graduate-school colleague of mine was beaten to within an inch of her life by her ex-spouse, a man against whom she had a restraining order. The day before he broke into her house and savaged her, he came to her house and killed her dog. This was the second incident I knew about where the mistreatment of a companion animal preceded violence against a woman. The first happened several years earlier, in 1991. My parents' friends' daughter, Nan Schiffman, was

brutally murdered by two men who had worked on a paint crew at her house. One of the men had done something to her dog, and she had complained to the men's employers. The men abducted, raped, and murdered Nan, then buried her body at an abandoned farm.

How do I link these experiences? To my mind, they are all about arbitrary and contradictory rules that are gender specific, about consumption, and about violent control. They are all, as well—and this is something I can only see now, in retrospect—about restoring the absent referent, Carol Adams' term for the way that language is used to remove actual bodies from discussions of the brutalization and consumption of bodies. So to reiterate and expound: I come from contradictory circumstances, a state both liberal and conservative, a family both permissive and dictatorial, the daughter of a father who treated me, in many ways, like the son he likely wished I was, but who always came up against his beliefs that girls and women should occupy certain confining spaces. So, here's the rub: as a teenager, I could drive a tractor and I knew a lot about cars, but if I swore or stayed out late, I'd get in trouble. I was expected to be smart and pretty, and for me, that was an impossible balance, to be cognizant of all the reasons why being pretty was a trap, to be able to articulate those reasons, and to be held to those expectations nonetheless. To hold myself to them and to punish myself for not adhering to either piece of the equation of beauty and brains. Hegemony is, after all, rule by consent.

Oh, and I was expected to eat meat.

To be pretty and smart in the South in the 1970s and 1980s, for me, at least, was to disappear, to make myself absent. To absent myself—my body—already rhetorically absent in the universalizing pronouncement of "he," via an eating disorder that overtook my life for over a decade.

I. Disordered Pronouns

I don't remember my mother's answer to the question about the universal pronoun of "he," or maybe she didn't have an answer, having always just accepted as truth the fact that femaleness, in the abstraction of generalization, simply ceased to exist, simply disappeared in the crush of overwhelming masculinity. But to this day I remember raising the question, knowing that there was some injustice in the negation, even as I grew more and more acquainted with what it meant to be negated. And that knowledge stuck.

When I went on that class trip to the sausage plant several years later, I'd already asked my poor parents a second question: Where does meat come from? Did the animals die naturally before we ate them, or were they killed? Again, I don't remember the answer, probably, this time, because whatever I was told proved woefully untrue in the blinding glare of the truths revealed to me that day in the processing plant. Lessons learned and then discarded: "he" is the universal pronoun because *it is*. Animals are violently killed and I eat them because *I do*. And then I didn't anymore, at least not those animals, at least not pigs, whose bodies I'd seen hung on hooks, gutted and waiting to be processed. Never those animals. Never again. Sausage was pigs, real, once-living pigs, the bodies of which were bigger than I was, the eyes of which, on that day, stared at me out of dead sockets. I started using "she" as my universal pronoun thereafter as well; I lost points on papers for doing so. I was consistently corrected, all the way through my undergraduate studies, but never stopped.

II. Disordered Eating

When I went to college at Appalachian State University, I became a vegetarian, fully and completely, and I started running. I lived in Boone, North Carolina, a tiny town at the time where nothing bad ever happened. I ran on backcountry roads; I ran at night. Running made me feel free. I was able to eschew eating some meat—sausage, for example—while I lived with my parents, but I couldn't make a case for not eating any meat without getting in trouble at home. My life up until that point had been, at least from the time I was about thirteen until I left at age eighteen, a struggle to gain some semblance of control of my body and intellect from my parents, who—with what I have no doubt were the best of intentions—continually wrested control away from me in their attempts to protect and care for me. Such circumstances are not unusual; I was the elder of two daughters, the one upon whom they had experimented, as parents must, with *how* to parent. They were by turns loving, demanding, and incredibly rigid; I, in turn, was a perfectionist and an overachiever, and was often profoundly angry.

The power struggles between my parents and me were more often than not about my body: what I wore, how my hair looked, how far my stomach protruded and why I didn't hold it in as was appropriate for a girl of my upbringing. Undoubtedly, then, food became for me, as it is for many girls like me, both an enemy and

a weapon; food was by turns a catalyst for unseemly and inappropriate appetites that threatened to overwhelm me and alternately
something that I could resist, the concrete substance through which
I demonstrated my will and strength. Not eating was a paradoxical
act of control, one that enabled my first clear acts of defiance even
as doing so undermined my health and sanity. The problem, at least
initially, is that I wasn't sure what I was defying.

But to be clear: becoming a vegetarian when I went to college
and asserting that identity when I went home to visit my family was
a manifestation of an awareness that fomented on that visit to the
sausage plant years before, that animals that become meat suffer and
die to feed us. I became a vegetarian out of a desire not to participate
in that suffering, but my vegetarianism also served as an assertion
of my own identity and an affront to my parents who didn't know
what to do with or how to feed a vegetarian daughter and who took
understandable offense at what they viewed as a rejection of their
care, their nourishment, and their heritage.

I am well aware of the ways in which women use vegetarianism as a so-called excuse to cut things out of their diets, and there
is a significant body of research on this subject, as chronicled and
detailed by my colleague and friend Hal Herzog on his blog at *Psychology Today.* What some research would seem to indicate is that
women cut meat out of their diets to lose weight; they claim to be
vegetarian in order to make an excuse for not eating certain things. In
this light, being a "vegetarian" is divorced from its ethical implications and becomes a way to mask disordered eating. Herzog notes an
interview he conducted for his recent book *Some We Love, Some We
Hate, Some We Eat: Why It's So Hard to Think Straight About Animals*, one woman claimed that "she became a vegetarian when she

was a teenager. Then she dropped the bombshell: Her vegetarianism was tied up with an eating disorder."

Okay, so my vegetarianism was also tied up with the eating disorder that fully manifested itself when I was nineteen, but I think that for women who find themselves in such circumstances, the connections between these two things—vegetarianism and eating disorders—are much more complicated than simply one serving as an excuse for the other. I know that in my case this reality is a profound truth. Not eating meat made sense to me, and I was not eating meat for ethical reasons; I have never doubted that. But along with not eating meat, I was left with a void with regard to *how* to eat thereafter. I was left without resources to enable one great leap in terms of my consciousness, care for nonhuman animals—my vegetarianism—to translate into self-care that could nourish and sustain a position that felt so unfamiliar and, in many ways, unsafe to me.

Think about it this way: if at age nineteen I was aware on some visceral level—and I was—of a kind of erasure of women and animals via tricks of language that render them absent, then I was not yet aware of the connections between such rhetorical violence and actual violence done to animals and women. I had no road map for making those connections or for knowing how to assert an alternate and independent female identity, no matter how much I wanted to do so. In the space of being a vegetarian whose prior existence had been predicated on the consumption of meat, and of being a fledgling feminist whose prior attempts at self-assertion had been effectively quelled, I found myself shuttling between a positive sense of self-assertion ("eating animals is wrong") and a negative internalization of learned helplessness ("so what do I do now?"). I started, quite literally this time, to disappear. And then women around me, women

I knew, women who were independent and self-actualized, disappeared as well.

III. A Timeline

1989: I become a vegetarian. Jeni Gray is abducted from the same sidewalk where I run every day in Boone, North Carolina. Her body is found two weeks later, raped and murdered. Daniel Brian Lee, the man who killed her, abducts another woman, Leigh Cooper Wallace—a fellow college student and runner like me—again from my running loop and rapes her. She escapes and identifies him. (He dies of a brain aneurysm in prison several years later.)

1990: *The Sexual Politics of Meat* is published.

1991: Steven Bishop and Kenny Kaiser rape and murder Nan Schiffman after she complains to their employers about their treatment of her dog.

1992: I graduate from Appalachian State University with a B.A. in English and start graduate study at East Carolina University, where I write an M.A. thesis on Tsitsi Dangarembga's *Nervous Conditions*, a novel about a young Shona woman named Tambu who goes to live with her English-educated relatives. Tambu's cousin, Maiguru's daughter Nyasha, develops an eating disorder, caught as she is between her English upbringing and her Shona culture—one defined by a diet based on meat and the other on a diet based on vegetables—and the weight of European and Shona patriarchal standards.

1993: My graduate school colleague's ex-husband kills her dog and then returns the next day to brutally beat her.

IV. Disempowering the Disorders

"Sexual violence and meat eating, which appear to be discrete forms of violence, find a point of intersection in the absent referent. Cultural images of sexual violence, and actual sexual violence, often rely on our knowledge of how animals are butchered and eaten."

—Carol J. Adams, *The Sexual Politics of Meat*

"When you have sex with someone strange—when you trap her, hold her down, get her under you, put all your weight on her—isn't it a bit like killing? Pushing the knife in; exiting afterwards, leaving the body behind covered in blood—doesn't it feel like murder, like getting away with murder?"

—Lucy Lurie in J. M. Coetzee's *Disgrace*

Sometime around 1994, I started seeing a therapist about my eating disorder. For six years, I had alternated between being anorexic and being bulimic, and I was quite literally sick to death of the whole business. The therapist recommended that I join an eating disorders group, which I did, despite that fact that I'm an incredibly solitary person and the thought of confessing my issues to other people was terrifying. Both the individual therapy and the group encounters helped me to be more clear about what I was doing and why I was doing it, and I was able to see that other women—and we were all women, of course—really did struggle with the same issues that affected me. But one thing seemed to distinguish me from these other women: I hated men, and they didn't. That hatred had been growing in me for a long time: I was certain that this eating disorder was the product of patriarchy; I just had no idea what to do with that knowledge except to hate—and to turn that hatred back against myself. I remember once during a group session, my therapist brought in a male colleague who was doing work on eating disorders. I got up and stormed out.

I found *The Sexual Politics of Meat*, hiding on a bookshelf in my own home, purchased years before by my then-boyfriend and now-husband, Jason. A brief preface: reading literature (and I mean fiction), for as long as I can remember has been the way that I make sense of the world. That's why I majored in English and continued in that field—literature is the lens through which I view everything, because, in many ways, fiction is truer than fact. I think Nadine Gordimer's point about this, made in *Living in the Interregnum*, her 1982 James Lecture presented at the New York Institute for the Humanities, gets at my feelings about literature: "Nothing I say here [about the state of apartheid South Africa] will be as true as my fiction." My study of literature has always focused on what it tells us about so-called minority voices—those of women, citizens living under oppressive regimes—as well as those who are voiceless in a traditional sense, namely, animals. And that study has always been deeply linked to my own activism as someone who has worked for both animal and human rights. Given these truths, I'm not sure why Adams' study had eluded me for so long, especially given that it had been hiding in plain sight for several years. And I'm not sure why I picked it up when I did, that fateful day in 2001, but I'm forever thankful that I did; reading it changed my life and my scholarship in ways that have been profoundly significant, productive, and therapeutic.

By 2001, I had gotten a grip on both my eating disorder and my hatred issues, but neither had fully abated (much to the dismay of Jason, who decided to live with me in spite of myself), despite years of hard work. When I found *The Sexual Politics of Meat*, I read it over the course of two days. When I was finished, I felt that for the first time in my life, someone had articulated for me all the missing connections that then allowed me to make sense out of the disjointed narrative of my previous experiences with regard to animals, eating, women, and violence.

Adams, like me, is a student of fictions and the various truths that they convey, and the texts that she analyzes in this work range from novels (her analysis of Mary Shelley's *Frankenstein* is a staple text in my graduate gender studies seminars), to historical documents, to multicultural myths, to television advertisements, all of which demonstrate the mythology of meat and the ways that a meat-based diet is not only cruel to animals but constitutes sexist and racist ideology. I wondered where this work had been back in 1992 when I had been doing that M.A. thesis on *Nervous Conditions*.

I decided very soon thereafter—and largely in response to my internalization of Adams' argument—that one of the most feminist things I could do would be to become vegan, so I did. This time, instead of having my animal-conscious dietary choice linked to an eating disorder, I was able to link it to a recovery of sorts. Jason had always said—and rightly—that I wasn't really a very good vegetarian; he called me a "meat avoider," because I wasn't really doing anything other than simply avoiding meat. Being a vegetarian, he said, meant eating *vegetables*. As a vegetarian, I ate lots of carbohydrates and processed junk. Remember: just because something is "vegetarian" doesn't necessarily mean that it's good for you. At that time, I hadn't really cared about what was good for me; I just knew that I didn't want to eat animals.

This time around, becoming vegan, I made a conscious choice to eat more fully and to eat better, to consume things that would make me healthy and strong, to eat food that was fresh, whole, and not processed. The goal was as much one of self-empowerment as animal liberation—and because the connections between those two things were now clear to me, I was able to be empowered by this choice. Becoming vegan, in its most feminist manifestation, meant doing something actively in response to a cultural stasis that dictated dietary behavior with which I simply did not agree. This time around, I was reacting in ways that felt fully conscious, and that consciousness has allowed me to eat—and live—more and better than I ever did before.

I started work on my Ph.D. in English at the University of Massachusetts in 1999, the same year that South African author (and later Nobel laureate) J. M. Coetzee published two works, neither of which I read until several years later. The first, *The Lives of Animals*, constitutes his 1997–98 Princeton Tanner lectures, a text that consists of two narratives about the fictional novelist Elizabeth Costello's animal rights lectures at fictional Appleton College. Over the course of the first lecture, she compares the slaughter of animals in industrialized societies to the slaughter of Jews during the Holocaust. The second, *Disgrace*, is a novel set in post-apartheid South Africa about, among other things, the rape of Lucy Lurie, a white, lesbian, vegetarian South African woman, by three black South African men who also shoot and kill the dogs that she kennels. Lucy's father, the disgraced former university English professor David Lurie, forced from his job after a questionably consensual sexual relationship with one of his undergraduate female students, moves in with Lucy prior to the attack— during which Lucy's rapists douse him with flammable liquid and set him on fire. These two works, in their attention to animal rights issues, are often considered companion pieces of a sort, and they, along with others of Coetzee's novels, became the basis for the dissertation that later turned into my first monograph, *Writing "Out of All the Camps": J. M. Coetzee's Narratives of Displacement* (Routledge, 2006).

When I started my Ph.D. in 1999, I was relatively certain that I would work on postcolonial women's literature; my M.A. coursework and thesis had been in the area of African women's writing, and I was inclined to continue that trajectory. My reasons were simple: texts make it into the canon—and are dropped from it—based in part on how much scholarly attention they receive. I wanted women writers from all over the world to be read, taught, and discussed. So one of the first two classes that I took my first semester at the University of Massachusetts was a seminar on Nadine Gordimer and J. M. Coetzee. Gordimer's work I knew; Coetzee I'd never heard of. I took the course for Gordimer, and I left convinced that I would write my dissertation on Coetzee, who in real life is a vegetarian and animal rights proponent. The shift took place perhaps because I stopped hating men as much, stopped holding some generic category of "man" any more accountable for the injustice in the world and in my own life than I held women—or myself, for that matter. Coetzee was a man, and the thought of writing about him and his work, I must admit, was for a long time hard for me to reconcile with my anger toward all men. But I chose to write about Coetzee's fictions because of the way that they engage with two things: animal otherness and women's positions—in South Africa and elsewhere—as boundary keepers, figures that often occupy the space of both dominated and dominating.

V. Now

I live in Asheville, North Carolina, and I teach nonwestern literature and gender studies at Western Carolina University. Jason owns a vegan restaurant, which means that—aside from the fact that I'm incredibly lucky and never have to cook, which I've never liked or been very good at anyway—I eat better than ever. *The Sexual Politics of Meat* continues to find its way into my scholarship and to inform my lived experience, and I consistently encourage others to read the book as well, to agree or disagree with its assertions, to engage with its precepts. The world continues to offer up injustices that are suffered all over—women continue to struggle for recognition and animals still die horrific deaths in the service of the mythology of meat. I continue writing, engaging with Coetzee's work and other texts via a theoretical framework that employs my learned and lived ethic. If there is one thing (and in truth there are many) that *The Sexual Politics of Meat* has taught me, it's that in and of themselves, books may not be able to change troubling realities. But they can provide us with road maps that make some of the connections we're missing, and in that way, they can help us to get where we're going.

Fish and Frog

Brother Knows Best

SARAH E. BROWN

$\mathcal{I}$ have idolized my older brother Asher since I can remember, and this admiration has often led to mirroring many of his actions and activities. Asher, six years my senior, was editor in chief of our high school's newspaper—it was a natural fit for me to follow in his footsteps given my strong proclivities for writing and editing. He enrolled in botany and music history. I did, too, and these were some of the best classes I took in high school. I chose to run cross-country when Asher did because, like him, I was equipped with a lithe frame that was well-suited to the pace of long-distance running.

Following in my brother's footsteps has led me to some unusual activities, like interscholastic wrestling. While there were no girls on my school's wrestling team, I was so inspired by my gangly brother's unlikely winning streak in the 132-pound weight class that I, an 80-pound sixth grader, convinced my science teacher, the middle school wrestling coach, to allow me to join the team. I practiced with two other girls who were 20 pounds heavier than me and sweaty pubescent boys whose tightly packed muscles intimidated but never *attracted* me.

In retrospect, my lack of sexual feelings while romping around with male peers in tight spandex was an early sign that I might not be heterosexual. I inevitably used this to my advantage. I distinctly recall winning a match against a boy at a local Episcopalian school by virtue of his intimidation regarding the fierce-eyed girl in a singlet poised to take him down. At an age when most girls in my class were toning down their assertiveness in order to appeal to boys, I felt no shame in expressing aggression in front of a boy.

My brother taught me about exploiting vulnerabilities in the legs, which ironically became the reason he had to quit. Two popped kneecaps and enough tears of worry from my mother led to his departure from the sport, and shortly after, mine.

At age ten, Asher decided to become vegetarian. My omnivorous parents were supportive of my brother's vegetarianism; my mother prepared meatless meals for him and non-vegetarian meals for the rest of us. I noticed that Asher eschewed meat, but as a young child I was never compelled to question it. After all, I was only four when he became vegetarian. It was something about him that I had grown up with, like his hair color or the galaxy of freckles on his face.

On vacation in France, outside our daily routines, Asher, then seventeen, decided that I as a twelve-year-old, was finally ready to handle a discussion about our incongruent diets. With the patience of a remarkable older brother, he simplified everything for me while he ate his salad amidst plates of fish and lobster my parents had ordered at a restaurant in the south of France.

Pointing to the array of lifeless sea creatures littering our table, he begged me to try to imagine the animals who lived and swam before ending belly-up on our table. He then implored me to imagine their slaughter, scooped into nets and tossed onto boats, flopping their bodies frantically until succumbing to suffocation.

"Look, do you really want to be responsible for innocent animals' suffering and untimely deaths?" my brother asked.

Sitting in the restaurant in France, directly confronted with the reality of what eating animals meant—turning living creatures into objects for consumption—I couldn't continue my old unconscious eating patterns. I pushed my seafood plate aside and devoted myself to my salad. From then on, I was convinced I would be a lifelong vegetarian. My brother's arguments made vegetarianism seem irresistibly logical, and I asked my mother to prepare meatless meals for two now.

Unlike his hand-me-down T-shirts and jackets that ended up in my closets, my brother's vegetarianism fit me well, and I made it my own. When he went off to college, Asher granted me access to his bookshelf, which included his treasured science fiction and war books, French novels, and dog-eared copies of classics we were made to read in high school. Many of his books collected dust in his absence, but when I reached the end of high school, one precious book on his shelf shifted everything in my world: *The Sexual Politics of Meat*.

The red cover immediately stole my attention. A striking image of a woman in a sexualized pose, with portions of her body demarcated as cuts of meat, was both familiar and disturbing. Its cover offered an immediate opportunity to consider the connection between the consumption of women and animals.

Reading the book at age seventeen, I realized that it was hypocritical for me to be vegetarian and not vegan, since I believed so deeply in animal welfare and human welfare (my primary reasons for abstaining from animal flesh). I knew that eating cows was out of alignment with my ethics after my brother helped me to see how meat comes at the price of animal suffering, but this text illuminated an entirely new way of understanding how animal agriculture of dairy products reveals the ways in which females are particularly exploited.

Understanding the mechanisms of privilege and power that reinforce the eating of animals helped me recognize how I, a woman coming into my non-normative sexual orientation, related to the animal agriculture industrial complex. As I uncovered universal truths about the connections between oppression toward women and animals, it was in no way coincidental that I came out as a vegan and a lesbian the year I turned eighteen.

In high school I had played hokey pokey in and out of the closet. I risked telling a few teachers and friends about my budding sexuality, but for the most part, I stayed safely in the confines of the shadows. I hesitated to reveal my sexual orientation to those around me because of fear. I was afraid that my minority status would make it harder to achieve my professional and personal goals in life. As a vegan woman, I was afraid to openly claim yet another non-normative identity. Before I came out to my family I awakened to the insidious realization that some activists have to separate or "pick" which causes to promote.

On my fall break during my freshman year at college, I met up with Asher in Manhattan where, for the first time, I introduced him to a girlfriend. I had already come out to my brother over the phone a few weeks into the school year, but this was the first female partner of mine he'd ever met. Though Asher frequently threatened to break the kneecaps of guys I dated during my experimental phase in high school, he was very kind to her and made it clear that he accepted our relationship.

My brother looked older than I'd remembered, a few laugh lines and some new gray hairs sprinkled in his dark brown coif. Since I was twelve, the year I became vegetarian and he went off to college, I spent less time with him. I cherished the rare vacations when he'd return from Los Angeles to visit.

Asher took my girlfriend and me out to dinner at Sacred Chow, a small vegan restaurant in the East Village. After macrobiotic steamed vegetable rice bowls washed down with chocolate soy milkshakes, we wandered a few blocks to Union Square. Amidst the city din and the pronounced stench of caramelized nuts sold by the vendor across the street, I told him about my journey from vegetarianism to veganism. I told him why I thought he should be vegan. Asher listened to my earnest discussion about why veganism was a more practical extension of vegetarian theory, how it was a feminist issue, and how I thought he ought to drop the dairy and eggs from his diet. Asher, usually the one to lead the way, listened to me pontificate for several minutes. He was quiet, and then asked me to give him some time to think it all over.

Three weeks later my brother called to tell me he was vegan.

As a vegan lesbian, I have straddled worlds that have felt unusual and uncomfortable. Just as omnivorous diets are often assumed, as a femme-looking lesbian, people often assume I date men. Being outspoken about my vegan diet has shown me the courage to be more upfront about my sexual orientation. "Don't you miss meat?" is a statement I've unfortunately fielded in both diet and sexuality contexts. Clearly, vegans have plenty of options when it comes to mock meat, and can get protein from any number of plant-based sources. Without going into too much detail, as a lesbian, I also feel that absolutely nothing is missing in the "meat" department of my love life!

Whenever I eat at a vegan restaurant, or go to a lesbian bar, I enjoy the ease with which I can express various aspects of my identity. In conventional restaurants and bars, it is becoming less of a challenge to order vegan things and to feel free holding my girlfriend's hand. As society changes, as states legalize gay marriage and strike down other laws that bar LGBTQ people from equal rights, I feel increasingly empowered to stand in my truth as someone unafraid to live an honest, decent life, which includes open, loving treatment of nonhuman animals, human animals, and myself.

At times, hiding one aspect of my identity has been necessary to survive. Coming out as vegan and/or lesbian is still a privilege in some areas of society. While studying abroad in Spain, my vocally homophobic host mother stifled my openness about my sexual orientation. I passed as straight in order to avoid harassment or getting kicked out of the house. Whenever this frustrated me, I could vent over email to my loving brother, who always understood and encouraged me to accept myself even in circumstances where I did have to hide. Ironically, my host mother did accept my being vegan—she adapted her Spanish cooking to tofu instead of fish, and delighted in the fact that she was able to save money since she didn't have to buy expensive meats for me. I recall many nights beginning with her delicious fried vegetables and uncooked plain tofu (which she pronounced toh-FU) followed by secret jaunts to lesbian dance clubs in the heart of Chueca. I have made peace with my choosing to hide for safety as a twenty-year-old studying abroad, but in the future, it is something that I hope never to have to do again.

All who are excluded in some way are potentially primed for the awareness of oppression in multiple contexts. As a lesbian vegan, I see all of the ways in which I am an "other" as guides on my path to support the liberation of all beings. The problems of speciesism, racism, transphobia, homophobia, and sexism are indeed vast, but there are practical solutions to these oppressive frameworks. Showing compassion toward all human and nonhuman animals simultaneously can involve promoting discrimination-free language, inclusive events, and serving plant-source-only food at all LGBTQ events. When I was the editor in chief of an LGBTQ publication in college, it made complete sense to me to ensure that all of our events were catered vegan. Veganism and queer activism merge deliciously.

Since first reading *The Sexual Politics of Meat*, the ripples in the pond of my life have been undeniable and highly significant. I chose to work at an environmentally focused nonprofit in the Bay Area after graduating from school, and then went on to work at a vegan holistic health center in Arizona for two years, where I met my partner. My partner and I are both vegan, write frequently on vegan topics for popular blogs, and are dedicated to spreading Carol Adams' messages of peace and compassion for all beings on the planet.

Adams' work is more relevant now than ever. We still live in a culture that is dominated by the sexual politics of meat. Examples abound in advertisements, the media, television, pop culture, and politics. Subverting these norms must occur at all levels of society. We must educate ourselves and our communities about the impact meat-eating and animal agriculture has on our health, animals, and the planet. To move away from exploitative practices in our culture toward women, it is clear that we must also move away from similarly exploitative practices in our consumption patterns.

It can be difficult to see the ways in which we participate in systems of oppression, and for many of us, the status quo benefits our privilege and therefore is more difficult to move away from. I am deeply proud of my brother Asher for choosing to live as an ethical vegan feminist, who extends compassion toward himself, me, and all creatures. His inspiration got me to consider vegetarianism, and turned me on to Carol Adams' work, which ultimately had a profound impact on my activist career and personal life. I am grateful that Asher has also been open to considering my perspectives, adopting a vegan diet that he has sustained ever since.

My brother and I currently live on opposite coasts of America. I cherish when my phone randomly buzzes, alerting me that my brother has sent a photo of a kale smoothie he has made in the industrial-grade blender I bought him for his birthday, or takeout from one of our favorite raw vegan restaurants in Los Angeles. When I moved to Philadelphia, Asher gifted my girlfriend and me with a Community Supported Agriculture (CSA) box containing a variety of delicious, locally grown produce. Through sharing wholesome plant-source-only foods, my brother and I remain connected through what sustains us: a love of veganism and each other.

Found Art, Found Hope

JASMIN SINGER

$\mathcal{I}$n 1990, when *The Sexual Politics of Meat* was first released, I was eleven years old, a sturdy and theatrical sixth grader who wore fluorescent colors and listened to *A Chorus Line* so frequently that my cassette tape wore out and needed to be replaced—not once, but twice. As it turned out, the arts, in all of their manifestations—which consumed my childhood and adolescence—would be both my saving grace and the impetus for catapulting me into the life I now lead. Ultimately, the arts would also become my chosen method for making my vision of the world come closer.

Perhaps surprisingly to some of her readers, I unquestionably credit Carol Adams for my initial interest in exploring the use of the arts as a means for changing the world. To me, her work, seen by so many as groundbreaking theory or controversial polemic, is, first and foremost, art. It is art that illuminated so much about the world, and about myself—and how I, as a woman, a feminist, and a person who is horrified about what is happening to animals, could make sense of it all.

Art and activism are two prevailing through-lines that have found their way into my life from the get-go. Even as a child who was remarkably ignorant of issues such as women's rights and animal rights, I did my best to speak up for those who couldn't. I recall using my Bat Mitzvah speech to talk about Ryan White, a boy who had died of complications of the AIDS virus—but only after he was expelled from his middle school thanks to the insistence of outraged, misinformed parents. Taking a stand against injustice is not uncommon for children, who have not yet been indoctrinated into the foibles of society. Perhaps that explains why, according to the Vegetarian Resource Group, the percentage of vegetarian children ages eight to eighteen (7 percent) is higher than the percentage of U.S. adults who are vegetarian (5 percent).

It is only as we are influenced by society and the media that we become not only victims of the idea of dominance—whether over women, animals, or other oppressed groups—but also perpetrators. We, as a society, willingly and mindlessly accept that certain groups fall beneath others in this hierarchal system that just *is*. The poison just seeps in.

But the poison is reversible. Once we start to squint our eyes and look at these things with a bit more discernment, we see that mind-sets like these are archaic and do not belong in an evolving and civilized culture. We owe an enormous debt of gratitude to the artists who help us see things more clearly and help us transform our minds, and then the world. Shrugging our shoulders and becoming complacent is not acceptable. In order to end this mind-set—this notion that "I am better than you and therefore can do whatever I want to you"—we cannot just wait patiently. We need to fight.

CONSUMED

I like to believe that my story is one of transformation.

I grew up in New Jersey, a middle-class white girl with all of the customary privileges and comforts that entails. Nevertheless, I was often lost, and I dreamed of escaping to New York City as soon as I could.

My early-to-bloom, plump body had become a source of self-loathing early on, and a "thing" for men to target with their words, their stares, and sometimes their hands. I recall walking home from school as a preteen, my backpack draped over one shoulder, when a car pulled over and the mustached man inside rolled down his window. I quickened my pace, but the car followed. "Hey, sweetheart," he yelled. "Nice tits for a little girl."

That experience was only the beginning of a long battle I faced with men making crude, sexualized comments regarding my figure, which, truth be told, would have been more appropriate on a full-figured woman ten years older than me. My large breasts and fulsome stomach were abominable to me, so much so that, not only did I follow the usual American teenage rite of off-and-on-again weight control diets but, at the age of sixteen, I underwent breast-reduction surgery.

It was a procedure I'd dreamt of having since I was in middle school, when my very grown-up breasts became the focal point of every adolescent male in sight, and made me the object of constant taunting and frequent abuse. Once, a group of boys tripped me in the hallway so that my books would spill, and as I bent down to gather my belongings, they poured water down my cleavage. I can see now that my immature voluptuousness was as confusing to them as it was to me, and they reacted to it in the way that society had suggested to them was appropriate. But that, of course, is hindsight. At the time, such behavior had its effects, and left its scars.

I countered this unrelenting bullying in any way I could—including cutting myself, which not only succeeded in taking the focus off of my emotional pain, but was also an attempt to annihilate my physical self. By the time I entered my teenage years, I was nursing my first dream of transformation. I would become an actress, a star. Yet my body seemed to stand in my way. I felt divorced from it, and I detested myself.

The antithesis of this disgust was the world of theater and art that pulsated around me and through me. I boycotted my senior prom (which is another way of saying I didn't have a date) to go to the Museum of Modern Art. I spent my weekends trying to secure rush tickets to Broadway plays, and I was always first in line at the stage door, waiting with bated breath for an autograph from a successful actor, and perhaps a stolen moment of validation. "You will be someone," I longed for one of them to say. It was this immersion into the counterculture world of theater and art that kept me going. That was the upside. The downside, perhaps, was that I was focused, very clearly and monomaniacally, on me and my dreams, and not on the world around me.

Despite this, thanks to the influence of a few empathic and insightful teachers—my role models—it still didn't escape me that I was able-bodied, monetarily comfortable, and by mere luck of the draw, came from a class, education level, race, and society that made me inherently advantaged.

One privilege of which I was acutely *unaware*, however, was that of my species. Though I decided to ditch meat when I was eighteen, it was not until years later that I allowed myself to have any consciousness about animals. At the time, my desire to become a vegetarian was more tied into the fact that I was seeking an identity, and "vegetarian" seemed to suit. Despite the initial shallowness of my rationalization to stop eating meat, it seems clear now that my decision to boycott the meat industrial complex was deeply, intimately related to my need to transcend the society that had tried to diminish me as a woman—an understanding I only gleaned years later.

TAKING OFF MY MAKEUP

By becoming a vegetarian, I gave up my unwarranted power over animals (on a visceral level, anyway; it wasn't until I became vegan that I *consciously* ceded that power). Meat, as I would later realize, is the embodiment of a patriarchal culture. It seems only natural in retrospect that as I stopped eating it, I also began to embrace a new ethic, one that made room for my true feminist self—a self that, in my case, included a strong love for women. Though I'm certainly not implying that when a woman becomes a vegetarian, she will also become a lesbian, I do think it's likely that her personal authenticity will become more fully realized. In my experience, the process of conforming to a patriarchal society had included repressing my personal sexuality. Thus, my feminism is very entangled with my lesbianism.

In addition to coming out as gay, I was "coming out" as the real me. I remember one activity in my acting studio class, in which each student was asked to do something to expose a deep part of themselves, making the point that, when on stage, we must be the most truthful and raw actor we can be. One classmate told the story of having sex in the park in broad daylight. Another classmate choreographed a dance routine that detailed his struggle with not only wanting, but desperately *needing*, to be on stage (a feeling so many of us related to). For my project, I sat at a desk in front of my class, took out a jar of cold cream, smeared it all over my face, and took off my makeup.

As my classmates—who gasped in astonishment—knew, I normally hid behind many impenetrable masks, including a literal one, pounds of makeup that resulted in frequent comparisons to Liza Minnelli. I proudly flaunted thick mascara, black eyeliner that extended to my temples, red lipstick, and drawn-on moles. This was "my look," and though in retrospect it seems so trivial, as I dismantled it in front of my peers, I unraveled another part of my true self.

Transformation frequently requires stepping out of your comfort zone just long enough to grow. As a little girl, in order to escape the bullies, I would visit a nearby wetland that was overrun with cattails. Though suburban New Jersey is hardly an enclave of nature, this little corner seemed somehow secret, giving me the peace of mind to stare unendingly at the sky, or loudly sing songs from *Annie*, or passionately recite scenes from *Family Ties*. One day, I saw a group of tadpoles, slimy and alien-like, swimming just feet from where I sat. I was amazed at these little creatures, and week after week, I caught glimpses of the tiny amphibians, watching with awe as they became loud, boisterous frogs. Their effortless evolution astounded me. Years later, as a college student working so hard to expose to my peers—let alone to myself—who I truly was, I like to think I was inspired by the tadpoles who bravely and naturally grew into themselves. At eighteen, I, too, finally felt myself begin to sprout legs.

PIECES OF MYSELF

Of course, life is seldom a simple road from bad to good. There are so many deviations along the way. A year later, I became part of an ugly statistic: I was one of the one-in-eight college students who is raped. While on a date with a thirty-five-year-old man whom I'd met at a bookstore, during an appropriately dreary and unrelenting thunderstorm, he forced himself on me, despite my verbal and clear lack of consent. When he was finished, I quietly stumbled through his house, picking up the pieces of my outfit which had been strewn about in the struggle, and quietly left for home, to try to pick up the pieces of myself.

Thankfully, with much help from others—as well as my many journals of bitter, depressing, and ultimately hopeful poems—I managed to put myself back on track. I was warier, but still eager to live an honest and present life, and to be true to myself, and my inner tadpole. As previously planned, I moved to New York City to finish college and pursue my dream of being a frog—that is, an actor.

My first job after college was with an AIDS-awareness theater company. I performed plays for students in mostly inner-city New York schools focusing not only on AIDS awareness, but on LGBT rights, teen pregnancy, sexual abuse, and domestic violence. Following our performances, as trained actor-educators, we were each responsible for teaching a classroom full of students. Looking back, it's clear that as much as I was teaching, I was also actively learning, and using that learning to heal myself.

Somehow, it seems only natural that at this moment in my life, through a colleague at this progressive theater company, I met a vegan. Though I had been a vegetarian for many years, I had never before given any thought to the dairy and egg industries and, for years, I had mindlessly consumed mostly cheese omelets and pizza. Whenever it was necessary to announce my "dietary choices"— which is how I would have described it—I would say, "I'm a vegetarian, but not the mean kind."

It was not long before my friend was showing me footage of factory farming. As the story goes, I quickly became a vegan. My worldview rapidly shifted, as did my perception of where I fit in the grand scheme of things. My on-and-off depression that I'd had since childhood disappeared, replaced by a profound knowledge that getting stuck in my own ego for too long was counterproductive, because there was indeed a hidden universe of suffering that was begging for all of our attention, mine included. I welcomed into my life a fierce determination to use every day I had to speak up for animals.

I was twenty-four, and a newly hatched vegan, when a friend handed me a copy of the recently published *The Pornography of Meat*. That book, rather than the earlier *The Sexual Politics of Meat*, was my introduction to Carol Adams, though I soon devoured both. I never looked back. The images haunted me, and transformed me from an activist who was just finding my voice to one who was ready to take action. For months—well after finishing them—I carried these books with me wherever I went, and could frequently be found on the subway rereading passages or gazing in unending horror at the images. Frequently, a stranger next to me would catch a glimpse of an oppressive ad Adams had dissected, such as the one on the front cover of *The Pornography of Meat*—a cheeseburger with a woman's bare legs popping out beneath it, complete with stilettos, touting the catch phrase, "100% PURE BEEF!"—and remain riveted, almost hypnotized, until she reached her stop.

And for me as well, it was Adams' brilliant and unabashed use

of visuals that had an even greater impact on me than did her rheto-
ric. As I flipped through page after page of what she describes as
"body chopping"—where an ad shows dismembered bodies—I was
reminded of my childhood tormentors. All they could see when they
looked at me, a twelve-year-old child, were my breasts. I was something to be consumed. My body was not mine. By sharing images of
other female bodies that had been deconstructed for male consumption, Adams showed me how my own suffering was linked to wider,
oppressive social norms. For the first time, I was able to see that the
disconnect I felt from my body as a young woman had resulted from
residing in a culture in which it is normal for women and animals to
be regarded not as sentient and autonomous creatures, but rather as
"meat."

While Adams' pictures disturbed me in incoherent ways, what
she did with them not only brought me coherence but also relief—
even revenge. All of these images were intended, by the advertisers,
to convey the message that women and animals are the same, things
to be "swallowed." But Adams transformed that message into something else entirely, making the images convey a story that was not
about animals, not about women, and not about me. Instead, it was a
story about the motivations and the mind-set of the people who created the images. She was revealing the malevolence that lay beneath.
She was having the last laugh.

Even though, by the time Adams' work reached me, I was
already vegan, the way she co-opted these visuals and turned the
tables allowed me to once again see things in a whole new light.
I recall staring at these images of body chopping and thinking of
the breast reduction surgery I'd eagerly undergone as a teenager.
Though obviously elective and entirely consensual, the main under-
lying reason for my surgery—aside from back pain—was to manip-

ulate my body to make it conform to what I was "supposed" to look like, and reduce its impact on those who were intent on dismembering me visually. For them, like the women and animals in Adams' collection of ads, I was faceless.

Beyond my surgery, the self-mutilation I had inflicted—literally cutting myself—was, in many ways, an attempt to fragment my own body parts. Though used as a way to distract from emotional pain by inflicting physical pain, I cannot help but think that I was so disconnected from my own body that I, too, was beginning to see myself as a piece of meat.

Years later, it was the work of Adams that further dismantled my hardened, self-loathing exterior, allowing me to blossom into the activist and feminist that lay beneath the masks. Though I had immersed myself in a world, a career, and a life of the arts, Adams' use of imagery as a means to create change dramatically expanded my understanding of art. The arts were no longer merely instruments of personal expression; they were a means of inciting social change. This is partly why I now consider what Adams compiled to be found art.

Though I realize that when most people think of Adams' work, they do not immediately think "art," there is no doubt that, for me, her unique and compelling way of taking sexist and oppressive images and contextually subverting their meaning is, indeed, a deeply real and honest form of art. What Adams at first dissects, she ultimately liberates, and then turns on its head.

Objects can become "found art" when they are put in a context that transforms them. By putting these images into *The Pornography of Meat*, or *The Sexual Politics of Meat* slideshow, Adams contextualizes them in a way that not only changes their meaning, but allows them to speak truth to power. As with other found art, the advertisements themselves remain literally unaltered. And yet, within the context of "a feminist-vegetarian critical theory" (the subtitle of *The Sexual Politics of Meat*), they are anything but.

Looked at through this lens and from this vantage point, it is clear to me why Adams' collection has so deeply seeped its way into my psyche, my activism, and my worldview. There is something so wonderfully subversive and empowering about dismantling "The Man," and Adams manages to do it twice—by showing the popularized, hidden-in-plain-sight, oppression and marginalization of both women and animals.

ALL THEIR LITTLE THOUGHTS

After I read Adams' work, and learned more about animal agribusiness, the parallels became clearer and clearer. When I read about the "rape rack"—the industry's term for the contraption that dairy cows are attached to so that they can be forcibly inseminated and impregnated—my own attack came vividly back to me. As a tormented child, I was called a "fat cow," and as a young adult I was raped—much like female cows are year after year. The connections were finally impossible for me to ignore, and my decision to be vegan became indelible. How could I stand up for other marginalized groups—such as the LGBT community, victims of the HIV virus, and even survivors of rape—yet continue to support the oppression of animals by literally funding the industry and buying its products? And what did I even mean when I said "its products"? The milk I was consuming was not a product of the dairy industry—or, at least, not originally. It was a product of the cows who produced it from their bodies, for their babies. I recalled watching the footage of factory farming, of cows screaming, and I thought of the many times I would leave rehearsal from a play that focused on rape, and get some ice cream on the way home—a "food" that was the byproduct of, in essence, rape.

I also thought of my own date rape, and how it had haunted me for so many years. I thought back to the evening of the attack, feeling so helpless and afraid, so thoroughly violated. Yet unknowingly, I had continued to be complacent—one could even say *proactive*—in helping to fund animal agriculture, a dark and ugly world that profited from, among other horrors, "rape racks." My head spun.

A few years ago, when my partner's cat Fergus unexpectedly died, as she mourned, she kept saying over and over again, "all his little thoughts . . ." As so many of us animal advocates do, she was looking at it from the animal's perspective—not the human's. "All his little thoughts" is a sentiment that I think about frequently. It has stuck with me almost annoyingly, like a song I can't get out of my head. When I think of the number of animals who are mindlessly and heartlessly forced into the kill line, where they frequently protest and shake with fear, I cannot help but think, "all their little thoughts!"

We, as humans, are taking away everything that is of value to these animals. First, we take away their freedom. Then we take away their dignity, their least bit of comfort, any chance they have of pleasure or joy. Finally, we take away their lives, putting a final end to all their little thoughts, as if they have no meaning whatsoever.

CREATING CHANGE THROUGH CREATING ART

Before we can change the world for animals, we must have a vision, a feeling, an understanding, at least an inkling, that something big is awry and that the only thing that will put a stop to it is something equally big. Carol Adams epitomizes that line of thinking. She took images that were originally intended to convey the message that women and animals are underlings, and usurped them, using them instead to expose abuse of unjust power. In the boldest of all her tactics, Adams appropriated these images to serve good, rather than evil. She raised eyebrows and ruckuses. Some feminists began to consider animal rights issues; some animal rights activists (like me) began to embrace feminism. Some people stormed out, some stormed in, some just got stormed upon.

What Adams created with *The Sexual Politics of Meat*, and what she so meticulously displayed with the slideshow and *The Pornography of Meat*, embodies and inspires what my partner, animal rights law professor Mariann Sullivan, and I have tried to create with our "indefatigably positive" strategy for changing the world for animals, through the work of Our Hen House—the organization we founded in January 2010. When you look at the ways in which oppression is alive and well for animals worldwide, both human and non, when you pause to notice the modern day holocaust, the innumerable injustices, there are so many reasons to be furious and depressed. Certainly for me, those emotions still seep in, and sometimes (perhaps more than sometimes) they even inform my worldview. But, strategically speaking, if we want to be in this fight for the long run, if we are angling for a more just and less cruel society, then focusing on positive ways to create change, turning the tables and retaining our power, transforming ourselves and the world around us, is a must.

It was that desire to empower ourselves and others to incorporate activism into our everyday lives—whether we're students, teachers, office workers, business owners, media mavens, artists, whatever—that ultimately gave rise to Our Hen House. You might say we started it out of frustration, because we began to notice how easy it was to pass the buck when it came to creating change for animals, waiting for the bigger organizations to circulate a petition or start a donation drive. Though those campaigns can be very important, so much more is needed. In order to change the world for animals, we need to create a huge shift in society and change the way consumers consume. To do that, we each need to use all the resources at our disposal—our social circles, talents, interests, and visions. To channel all of that into a unique way to change the world is, I believe, the best way to take advantage of our time on this planet.

Taking my own advice, I originally decided that Mariann and I should just start a podcast. I figured that with my theater training, combined with Mariann's insight, philosophical smarts, and expert take on animal law, we would strike a good balance. It turned out that, at the same time as I was planning the podcast, Mariann was thinking about starting a blog highlighting vegan businesses. So we decided to blend the two ideas, and throw in several more categories for the blog, each one showcasing different ideas or opportunities for everyone to get involved with changing the shape of things.

The idea for one of those new sections hit me like lightning: we would start a section called "Art of the Animal," highlighting the work of artists of all kinds who speak up for animals through their art. One thing led to another, and our little blog and podcast soon added a video production unit. The most exciting part all along has been the realization of how deeply it resonated with people, and how quickly it grew, demonstrating how thirsty so many people were for a resource that offered them "a place to find our way to change the world for animals," which is also our tagline. Soon, we became a 501(c)(3) nonprofit organization, and just this year, expanded to a multimedia online magazine.

The most popular leg of what we produce is our podcast, making my inner pundit very happy. Proudly, we have produced a one-hour episode every single week since our inception, and we are still going very strong. The podcast, which is very much like a radio show, allows us to hash out some of our feelings and thoughts regarding animal rights issues, lets us learn from some of the greatest movers and shakers out there—including ethicists, professors, celebrities, business owners, students, religious leaders, lawyers, and yes, artists—and allows us a platform in which to discuss animal-related current events. As always, we strive to remain "indefatigably positive." And of particular significance to me, we continue to place a strong emphasis on the arts.

What do I mean when I say "the arts"? Perhaps my view is different than that of some people. After all, we each have to answer that question for ourselves. "Art only happens when the viewer says it happens." So said visual artist Sue Coe, whose harrowing, educational, and stunning drawings frequently offer detailed depictions of exploited farmed animals. Coe said this in a video I directed for our Art of the Animal series. The potentially perfect marriage of the arts and animal advocacy—a marriage that, for me, commenced when I learned about Adams' work—has not been explored nearly as much as it should be. Hopefully, Our Hen House can play a vital role in bringing them together more effectively, while at the same time providing inroads for those who want change the world for animals.

THE MEAN KIND

I like to think that I continue to learn from my mistakes and continue to transform. When I used to introduce myself as "a vegetarian, but not the mean kind," I now recognize that I meant "not the activist variety," or, more likely, "not vegan." I would sneer as I said it, too, sharing a knowing moment with whomever I was talking to. "Don't lump me in with them!" (In hindsight, I now choose to recognize the term "the *mean kind*" as an unintended irony, a satisfying play on words. Freud would have a field day.)

Had I given even a brief pause to consider why vegans tend to be a vocal bunch, why they abstain from milk and eggs, or what the ethical implications of these products were, perhaps I would have found my path much sooner. But my own personal wall of denial got in the way. Thankfully, when it did come time for me to scrutinize the reasons to become a vegan—the countless ethical imperatives and benefits to adopting a totally plant-based diet—I was finally open to it. And this process goes on. Remembering that journey makes me ask: What injustice am I unwillingly participating in because I am going along with the status quo? In what ways am I blind?

We evolve, we change, we speak up. Tadpoles become frogs without effort. Humans, an intensely social species, often find transformation only when another person leads them to it. For me, as was true for my whole life, opening eyes, planting ideas, and shifting perceptions, all starts with art. It was the impetus for Our Hen House, and is the driving force behind my activism.

Found art is a medium that is inherently subversive, a way of "flipping the bird" at a mostly unjust, asleep society—and a way to begin to create change. When she wrote *The Sexual Politics of Meat* and *The Pornography of Meat*, Adams masterfully flipped the bird. Nowadays, each time someone else picks up a copy of either book, she flips it again.

My story is one of transforming from a bullied, awkward adolescent who loathed her body into a confident, still-changing adult with many moments of happiness reaching me each day. Adams' work, too, is about transformation. She transforms images that are meant to deride animals and women into images that illuminate the oppressive mind-set of those who would deride animals and women. She transforms these images from a commentary on animals and women to a commentary on the commenters.

I like to imagine a young feminist in a bookstore somewhere, coming across either *The Sexual Politics of Meat* or *The Pornography of Meat*, opening it, squinting her eyes a little, and then perhaps frowning and cocking her head a bit. The turkey sandwich in her bag suddenly seems less appetizing, and that tiny voice in her head that occasionally chirped "vegan" so quietly she could barely hear, somehow sounds louder. It all starts to come together. This young woman in the bookstore looks up, a new determination creeping in, a deeper understanding and a firmer grasp of justice—and of injustice.

That is the power of art. That is the power of the work of Carol Adams. That is, right there, how to change the world.

Special thanks to Mariann Sullivan and Gena Hamshaw.

Woman

Eat Chocolate Have Faith in Women

LAGUSTA YEARWOOD

I'm a misanthrope who interacts with the public all day long. I'm a hardcore vegan who makes fancy chocolates for a living. I'm an anarchist who owns my own shop, situated in a building that I own. I'm a pessimist who wakes up every day happy and joyful and wild with desire to get to a job I adore.

Like Walt Whitman, I apparently contain multitudes. But the contradiction that people want to talk about is the one that makes me livid every time it's mentioned (almost always by women about to buy chocolates). I make chocolates all day and all night—every day and every night—and I'm five-foot eight and weigh 108 pounds.

My college women's studies training did not in any way prepare me for how to gracefully answer the women—women! My people! My allies!—who ask me my "secret" each and every day: How do you stay so skinny, being surrounded by chocolate all the time?

"Honestly, The Question is making me hate women," I said to a friend the other day. It felt wonderfully awful to admit it. Goddamn *women*, with their constant need for approval and validation and secret smiles from me, the shopgirl, that their "decadent" and "sinful" desires for organic, fair-trade, vegan truffles are okay.

Before I had the shop, I didn't interact with many of these women. Most of my girlfriends have, as my mother's generation would have put it, "had their consciousnesses raised." It's not that we don't ask for honest appraisals of what our asses look like in those jeans or if that skirt is too short or too tight, but it's more that we don't conflate being as skinny as possible with looking as good as possible. My girlfriends—straight, gay, transgendered, fat, young, old, whatever—we want to look *good*. We are farmers, chefs, nonprofit slaves, radical lawyers, professors, artists, perpetual students, doulas, mothers, musicians. We aren't humorless feminists who believe looking damn sexy makes one a tool of the patriarchy—we've just been lucky to grow up in a tolerant enough environment to know that what constitutes damn sexiness is, and should be, defined differently by each woman (and man, but this piece is about women, so for now—and also maybe for the next millennium or so, too, okay? Reparations!—who cares about men).

Let me back up, though: *these women?* Did I really just say that? Ugh, how awful. I don't want to stand apart from the women who ask me the question. I want them to be my allies. But I just don't understand them one fucking bit, to be honest.

Books like *Skinny Bitch*, which promote veganism while using the exhausted and exhausting tropes of one body type being the only acceptable body type all women must aspire to don't really help the cause. In my view, they create vegans who lack any sort of awareness of the broader reasons to stop eating animal products and instead treat veganism as a diet, which most women will abandon if it doesn't immediately "work" for them. Fifteen years ago Carol Adams taught me that I need not throw my feminism under the bus for my veganism, and I don't see why I should now.

Here's my thing. Women and food: it's the oldest story around. A woman needs food to live.

Here are the facts as I, a chocolatier and most definitely not a nutritionist, understand them:

Who knows why I'm skinny? Who knows why anyone is anything? I've always been skinny, and only in the past fifteen years or so have I gotten any curves at all.

One reason I weigh what I do is because, let me just admit it, this strong woman is seriously lacking in muscle. Rolling truffles all day long is pretty good aerobic exercise, but it doesn't exactly build strength. And working twelve hours a day doesn't leave much time for strength training.

What I know is true is that women carrying a little (or a lot, depending on how your body is made) of fat around our stomachs and thighs and asses is an evolutionary success—fat stores translate to survival of the species, quite literally.

Truth be told, I've always been on good relations with my body. I've had some hard times in my day, and my body, my self, my innermost and outermost two beings, were always there for me.

When I was a kid and things were bad—my father screaming in a terrifying way next door, me absolutely certain he was going to kill us all—I sat in my bedroom and hugged my knees because, truly, my knees were the only huggable, lovable, friendable thing in my life. We had to stick together, this body and me. We were all we had. Mercifully, I didn't go through that awful thing most girls go through during puberty, where their body becomes an other to be hated. I didn't mind, terribly, anything my body did. Hairs and blood and all that, what can you do? We're still in this together. My body has always been my pal.

So how do I not contribute to our culture's insane fetishization of body types like mine, while, well, walking around in my body all day? How do I answer the question?

One thing I could say: there have been times when I've been healthy, and times when I haven't been—and my body has always looked the same. It seems like such an obvious point, but: someone's weight is not a reliable indicator of their overall health.

But *health* is not what someone is talking about when they off-handedly say, "How can you be surrounded by chocolate all day, and be so skinny?"

They are saying a lot of things, and one of them is that old saying about never trusting a skinny chef. How can someone angular and vaguely sour (I'm afraid I'm a bit of both) create true indulgences? Being skinny is all about self-deprivation, right? And good food is all about indulgence?

I'd say no to both—good food is about *nourishment*, in a literal way (it's needed to stay alive) and a quasi-spiritual way (good food feeds the soul). A dark chocolate truffle to round out a farm-fresh home-cooked meal, a caramel or two or fifteen after a stressful day— these are everyday treats that make life wonderful, not secret indulgences that we have to keep in check and make ourselves feel guilty about, lest we become gluttons.

But back to trust. There's something about trust in the question, isn't there?

I trust food.

We've gotten to such a sad place in our society that so many women, women chronically on diets, assume that to be around food means wanting to eat food. I don't want to eat when I'm not hungry. I love eating so much that eating when not hungry seems somehow treasonous, like getting a love letter and not even reading it.

But I understand the temptation to eat when food is there (an inclination I suspect many dieters have) because it's an inclination I had for many years for the opposite reason: as a kid I really didn't eat very much at all, because sometimes there just wasn't that much to eat. We ate a lot when we had food, because we didn't know what tomorrow would bring. It took me years and years to realize that food insecurity is, hopefully, not coming back into my life any time soon. I don't need to hoard food or eat like there's no tomorrow. Food is safely here, and the food is a world of warm, sheltering arms holding me. Food has always been my friend.

Getting back to the question. I feel like I'm subtly trying to answer the question (I only eat when I'm hungry!) when *the answer isn't what matters*.

Where the question comes from, is what I'm ramblingly trying to get to.

I don't want my joyful little chocolates to make anyone feel bad about themselves, or guilty, or naughty (except in a kinky way). I want my chocolates to be a celebration of life, of diversity, of happiness and wonder at what the earth can produce.

I don't want my chocolates to have anything to do with patriarchy. The "why are you so skinny" thing is, at its root, about the commandment we all have in our society, women more than men, but men, too, to be skinny at all costs. That old chestnut.

What I want to say is: "Hey, your question implies that skinny bodies are superior, and I reject that assumption! Hooray for size diversity, for health and happiness in all forms! It's a coincidence that I'm skinny, just as it's a coincidence that other women aren't, and we all deserve chocolate! Your question implies, also, that chocolate is a forbidden treat to be rationed out, and my dark chocolate, with its savory edges, with its stone-ground goodnesses and nibs and chilies and all the rest, is more akin to ancient Aztec chocolates that were a savory part of a meal, rather than the gross sugar bombs that are mainstream contemporary American chocolate! Chocolate for all! Here's to health and diversity and loving who we are! Here's to self-love! Here's to DESSERT!"

But more than that, since that's too many words anyway, I want to take these women's hands, and just look into their eyes, and *tell them they're okay*. I want to restore their essential self—their soul, I guess. Under patriarchy, each woman lives behind a veil of expectations. Behind that veil is the absent referent—the real person. Not wanting to participate in a system of oppression is why I'm a vegan, why I'm a feminist, why I'm a small business owner. I try to stay clean. It's impossible, but I still try. In my shop, I want women to just be women—not compared or abstracted or expected to be any sort of idealized type or archetype. I just want them to enjoy what I've made for them.

This, too, is impossible to convey in the lighthearted way in which the question is always asked. So what I do these days is simply to look into their eyes and smile.

Bodies are bodies, what can ya do. What can I get for you today?

Getting to Vedge

KATE JACOBY

*I*n the late spring of 2012, I arrived at work much like I do every morning. I fell into my normal pattern—firing up the ovens and getting our bread baking, toasting nuts and sifting flour, getting our ice creams churning. Late morning shifted into the early afternoon as the phones start ringing and the rest of the kitchen crew arrived. More of my same routine: placing orders, interviews, and emails. And just like any other day, I spent time reviewing the reservations to see which new guests would be joining us for the first time that evening and which regulars would be returning. I noted that my good friend Vance Lehmkulh had a reservation. It was always good to see him, but there was nothing particularly special about his coming in that night. Or so I thought.

Flash forward to 8 P.M. that evening. Our bar was bustling and lots of people were coming and going. I made eye contact with Vance and said hello. Then he said to me, "Kate, I'd like you to meet Carol Adams." All of my outgoing, front-of-house, restaurant banter skills flew out the window. I was completely speechless. We've had various celebrities in our dining rooms over the years, and I've never been at a loss for words. But this was a personal hero of mine who had just come through our doors. I pulled it together, shook Carol's hand, and managed to say something about being very honored to have her in my restaurant. So much for a typical day at Vedge.

It's been more than a decade since I've thumbed through my copy of *The Sexual Politics of Meat*. I haven't had to review its pages because, for me, it was just that powerful the first time around. So instead of being parked on my bookshelf, it's jumped from peer to friend to relative to coworker, running a circuit through like-minded and unlike-minded people whom I know would find the book, at the very least, thought-provoking. It wasn't until Vance brought Carol to dinner at Vedge that I rang up the last person on the chain and shook her down for my beloved copy. I still couldn't believe that I had just served dinner to one of the most respected voices of my impressionable college years.

I am the co-owner of Vedge restaurant in Philadelphia. Together with my husband Rich Landau, we have grown what started as his modest lunch counter Horizons Café in the suburbs of Philadelphia in 1994 into an exciting dining destination in one of the country's fastest-paced food towns. There are a few spectacular vegan restaurants across the country, and I am proud to count Vedge among them. Our current location, opened in the fall of 2011, is a gorgeous historic brownstone on Locust Street, the former home of the Princeton Club. Our diners are both from around the globe and from around the corner. They are strict vegan and they are hunters. They wear super-chic, eco-friendly vegan shoes, and they wear furs. They are lefty, liberal community organizers, and they are high-paid pharmaceutical reps. But however our guests live their lives, I never forget what an honor it is for me to make my living doing what I do. In small ways, and sometimes in very big ways, Vedge is showing people that a plant-based diet is a delicious and inventive choice. Yes, it's great for animals. Of course, it's great for human health. And yeah, think of all the grandchildren—it's an obvious choice for the planet. But at Vedge, our number-one mission is to inspire people about just how delicious and sensually satisfying vegan food is. Actually, we've come to calling it a vegetable restaurant rather than a vegan restaurant, focusing on the food rather than on the lifestyle. And that decision, that matter of syntax is, in my opinion, very much a result of my take on *The Sexual Politics of Meat*.

AS I CHILD, I never dreamed of becoming a pastry chef or restaurant owner. My aspirations were all over the place: singer, accountant, ice cream scooper, veterinarian. One that should have perhaps set off some alarms was a short-lived goal to become a director of a movie of naked men playing volleyball. The most shocking part of that fleeting idea was that it came to me at a very young age. I never understood the gender imbalance of nudity in movies and advertising, and that has stuck with me throughout my life.

So from elementary school onward, I was very much a "women's libber," as my mother described me. As I got a bit older, I grew very independent and proud, never blindly accepting the idea that boys should pay for me or open doors for me. Having been raised Catholic, I was very disappointed when I could not be an altar boy. (The church I attended as a child changed the rules one year after it was too late for me.) Nonetheless, this "women's libber" was not afraid to set foot in the kitchen. I loved baking alongside my mom and grandmother, and I was enamored by the stories they told me of the Christmas holidays at their house a generation earlier. Friends and family from the neighborhood would stop by and devour platters of homemade pierogies, coleslaw and potato salad, freshly baked cookies and *chrusciki* (Polish crullers). Here I learned to bake with my heart—how dough should feel, what a pinch is. My grandmoth-er's recipes on little index cards just listed ingredients; it was up to me to know how much, how long, and at what temperature. I was very intimately connected to food and what it does for family. I learned how important rituals are and how valuable time around the table can be.

So imagine this family scene being interrupted by vegetarian-ism. Well, that's what happened when I was about sixteen years old. It could have been worse. My family meals were already somewhat health-bent due to my father's heart condition. He had suffered a heart attack and survived bypass surgery, and I subsequently found myself able to whip up bran muffins blindfolded with one hand tied behind my back. So naturally, I was able to convince my mom that a vegetarian diet would have less fat and cholesterol. But protein was still a big issue. I became a very enthusiastic, budding chef who was more than eager to show how protein could be obtained from other sources, and how to make it fun and exciting, too. Avocado rolls in my lunch box? You bet!

When I left for college, the stage had been set. After a quick semester in the business school at Georgetown University, I worked my way into a double major in sociology and French with a heavy dose of women's studies coursework. I read a book about Monsanto; I interned at a domestic violence center; I performed in *The Vagina Monologues*; I lived in Dupont Circle; I even interned at a Catho-lic missionary agency that advocated for condom use in Africa and allowing priests to marry in South America. My world was turning upside down. And I was loving it.

In the middle of all this, I found Carol Adams' *The Sexual Poli-tics of Meat*. There were many texts I read in college that were provocative and enlightening, but this one stood out. She focused so many of my own arguments and perspectives in such a powerful way. All my hotheaded, pissed-off anger and isolation was beginning to be explained. And she did so in an intelligent and well-documented way. Why were my animal rights buddies acting like sexist jerks? And why were some of the girls at *The Vagina Monologues* auditions eating corned beef sandwiches? Two of my most important beliefs about feminism and animal rights—ones that literally defined me and helped me identify myself—were fused together seamlessly.

Best, or perhaps worst, of all, she explained the entrenchment; she made me understand the magnitude of the mainstream indoctrination into the dominant worldview. Discrimination against women can't be fully eradicated among people who eat steak with béarnaise sauce, and neither will supermarkets be stocked with vegan delights by a bunch of leering womanizers!

I walked out the Healy Gates of Georgetown University in 2001 feeling empowered—a little daunted in a David versus Goliath sort of way, but inspired to give my best effort, make my mark, and somehow do my best to change minds. I wanted people to understand that you do not need to accept the way the world is constructed around you. Nurture works both ways. If people can be indoctrinated one way, they can be redirected in another. Just how I would go about this grand plan was yet to be seen, but Carol Adams definitely helped light my fire.

AFTER COLLEGE, I tried out a few career paths: test coordinator for a fair housing agency, English teacher to French high school students, and sociology Ph.D. student. But the job I enjoyed the most was working my first summer out of college at Horizons Café.

Back then, Horizons was a modest lunch-and-dinner operation in a strip mall in suburban Philadelphia. The clientele was fairly diverse for the local demographics, but there was a strong representation of health-conscious types: yogis, empty nesters on cholesterol meds, cancer survivors, rebellious teens and college students, and very fit professionals. The scene was fairly casual, too, though we pumped our heart and soul into the food. Every plate had to be perfect. Vegetarian cuisine at this time was still shrouded in carnivorous terminology: Jamaican BBQ Seitan Wings, Tofu Scallops, Cuban Nachos with Soy Cheese, and Sopa de Tortilla. Horizons clearly took a Latin approach to cooking in those days, but regardless, it was a magical time when vegetarian cuisine in general and Horizons in particular were gaining momentum.

That fateful summer, I was supposed to host at Horizons for the summer before taking off for France to spend at least a year working for the Ministry of Education. But, I'm not gonna lie, the man who cooked all that great veggie food at the vegetarian restaurant I had loved for so many years was really hot. Every day, he tore down the terrible stereotypes that people have about womanizing restauranteurs and misogynistic chefs. He led and inspired a highly motivated kitchen team and had a fantastic rapport with the front of house as well. He was smart, wise, and fun. These were all things I needed to round out my angst. He was the woman-respecting, vegetarian man who just might help eradicate discrimination in the supermarkets!

Slowly, my plans for graduate school morphed into something entirely different. I began working full-time at Horizons on the kitchen line. When Rich and I weren't cooking, we were dining out, reading about food, and traveling to experience new food cultures. My palate was awakened. I learned the fundamentals of cooking in the Horizons kitchen, unfolding the mysteries of some of my favorite dishes: the Pecan and Sage-Baked Seitan, served over wild mushroom duxelles with sautéed French beans and a Yukon potato puree drizzled with black olive tapenade; the Sopa de Tortilla, a vibrant avocado stew with pinto beans and shaved corn in a rich poblano chile broth; the Yucatan Spinach Salad, a tangle of spinach, tomatoes, hearts of palm, and creamy cilantro dressing with guajillo chile oil and smoked black olives.

Outside Horizons, our frequent traveling and dining out taught me so much about different food cultures, starting with Latin and Caribbean cuisine, then European and Asian. Lessons in French techniques, bold Spanish flavors, and subtle Japanese preparations offered new ways to approach food. I was also an eager student of restaurant service: wine and cocktails, table settings, restaurant design. We carefully studied how to create a hip, enticing restaurant scene, one that would have appeal to the mainstream regardless of the cuisine being served. Equal partners in our business life and our personal life, Rich and I became the ultimate veggie foodies in a meat-eating world, happy to translate everything we were learning to our guests.

DURING OUR RESTAURANT'S evolution and my personal career trajectory, there have been several key moments and lessons that have continued to shape me. One of the broadest themes I've encountered is the struggle of hypocrisy. I've seen this play out many times. One recent example occurred here in Philadelphia when a local bakery volunteered to sell their cookies at the zoo to help raise funds for a nonprofit childhood disease organization. The bakery happens to be an allergen-free bakery; they don't use eggs or dairy.

The vegan community pressed them to discontinue using honey, so they have technically become, in the eyes of vegans, a vegan bakery. When this vegan bakery decided to support one of their customers by agreeing to participate in this bake sale, the vegan community was outraged that the bakery would set foot in the zoo. A heated exchanged transpired online between one of the bakery owners and a local animal rights advocate. As an outsider, I was saddened to think about the bakery owner and her frustrations trying to explain herself to the angry vegan who was trying persuade his friends to boycott her shop. I understand the vegan community's perspective, but why throw her under the bus? Why can't anything ever be good enough? Why must we all live in fear of the vegan police?

Whether I'm judging myself or feeling judged by others, I know one thing: nobody's perfect. I'm talking about the vegetarian who eats turkey on Thanksgiving, and the strict vegan who justifies using vaccine. Who is one person to judge another on their commitment level? That's not rhetorical. I've heard that "Hell hath no fury like the wrath of a scorned vegan," and I have witnessed that over the years. I get it. It's sometimes a lonesome place being vegan. It's tempting to inflate your inner tube with self-righteousness to keep you floating above the heathens who have no self-control. But how do those annoying voices from above inspire those scoundrels to stop eating meat? Or for that matter, to stop whistling at young ladies? Or stop using the *N* word? Or to stop arguing for the defense of marriage? Again, not rhetorical—how does this work?

One way is to live in a bubble. Surround yourself by people who can constantly support you and encourage you. Like smoking cessation buddies, we can call on one another to set things straight and keep everyone in line. But this becomes some sort of Ivory Tower. We all have relatives at holiday tables who will try to serve us meat or coworkers in a lunch room who will roll their eyes when you tell them your son is wearing a tutu.

Another option: keep to yourself. Don't tell anyone else how to live and they have no place telling you what to eat or how to dress. I've met people like this. They seem very content, and in some ways, I strive for that self-satisfaction. It's presumptuous to think that I need to change the world. But I know myself, and it's horribly difficult to bite my tongue.

My solution has been to put every effort I've got into demonstrating a desirable lifestyle to others. I don't preach vegetarianism, and I don't preach feminism. Not to the masses, anyway. I have peers who support me and encourage me, and I try to do the same for them. And I've gotten very good at detecting open-minded people who are ready to receive some cues about lifestyle changes. But overall, I've found the most success and satisfaction by putting out a positive example. I try not to appear different or difficult. I don't want veganism or feminism to seem like a lot of work. If others will be inspired, it has to seem easy, rewarding, a no-brainer. They can't think it's full of sacrifice and discipline. Remember two things: people are creatures of habit, and people love convenience.

FOR ME, IN most ways, living a life that flies in the face of the dominant worldview is easy. That's not to say it comes without hard work, but the commitment to certain beliefs is simple. People ask me how I work with my husband; they tell me they would kill themselves if they had to work with theirs. Maybe it's because we met in a work environment, but I think it's because we respect each other and trust each other as equals. Sure, we know our personal strengths and weaknesses, and we divvy up certain responsibilities, but I'm left wondering why the others married if they would hate working together so much!

In our home life, we have a similar dynamic. It's driven by our personal preferences and not by predetermined gender roles. I love Christmas cards; it would never cross Rich's mind to write one. He loves home decorating and design; without him, I would probably not have a single picture on the wall! Some things we do together, like making dinner, and other things are more delegated. But what's important here is that we choose for ourselves what we enjoy doing and what we do best rather than arbitrarily do what the mainstream would have us do. My boobs don't get in the way of me taking out the trash, and last I time I checked his penis doesn't impede him from folding laundry.

In 2007, I gave birth to our son Rio Jacoby-Landau. He has taught me more about life in four years than I learned from anyone or anything else (Carol Adams included). I adored every second of being pregnant and used that time to present a positive example. I ran, held doors for myself, ate well and not too much, and worked right up until the night before I delivered. After the birth, I was back at work in two weeks with Rio in a sling. And Rich was by my side throughout, devoting the same love, time, and attention to our newest family member. Full disclosure: being a new parent was at times a most excruciatingly difficult experience; it was by no means all candy and roses. That said, being a parent, being a woman, being a mom: these natural roles are ones I cherish deeply and appreciate fully.

Raising a vegetarian child has been a breeze for us. Perhaps it's because both his parents are chefs and we own a restaurant, but our son has a very adventurous palette, and so far he keeps healthy and fit. He has some vegetarian classmates, and he doesn't seem to have any trouble assimilating with his peers. I do see daily examples of the mainstream indoctrination—picture books presenting happy images of farmers with their cows on sunny pastures, television commercials marketing plastic jewelry and makeup kits to three-year-old girls, young girls at the playground who are taught not to lift up their dresses while the little boys are free to run around in their shorts without worry. . . . There are so many moments in a young person's life, the vast majority of which occur in a very subconscious way, where examples are set and beliefs are reinforced. We like to think of ourselves as a highly intelligent species. Well, when we hear something or see something repeated again and again, it becomes part of our perception. It's how advertising works and how stereotypes are made. And I work hard to stay tuned in to much of what our son sees each day. I don't pretend I'll be able to shield him from everything forever. But I'm trying to provide some level of filtration during these early years in his life. To the best of my ability, I want to provide him with some very clear alternative world views.

SO I'VE LEARNED a few key things in life so far. At certain points, you're supposed to be a student, though some people slack off as they get older. Perhaps that's why there's a glaring difference between the feisty, angsty, invincibles you meet on college campuses and the complacent, glazed-eyed consumers pushing carts at big-box shopping centers. There's a contagious energy emitted from optimistic young people who are really seeing the world for the first time and feeling they have the power to reshape it. And there's a depressing threat posed by people who have erred on the side of caution a few too many times, choosing the road more traveled so that they might at least know what to expect, like it or not.

The key for any social change is to get those who have bought into the system to, little by little, become comfortable with a new worldview. I'm delighted when I see Silk soymilk ads on major network advertising blocks, and I love the fact that there are more and more female anchors on prime-time news shows. I love that my son doesn't question why some of his friends have two mommies. And I will never forget sitting through the second *Jurassic Park* movie pleasantly puzzled at the lack of explanation over the white scientist's black daughter. I was embarrassed that I questioned it, and proud that the director didn't think it was necessary to draw attention to it. Carol Adams hints at what the world would be like if the struggle to improve it were no longer needed. People wonder what happens when there's no more injustice to fight. Whatever happens, I don't think we should be afraid of it. I certainly don't think we'll all be boring to one another. I don't think we need to have darkness to see light.

I see my path in life as an evolution, and looking back, each step makes sense to me. I believe my eight-year-old self, the one who wanted to film naked men playing volleyball, would give a thumbs-up to my thirty-two-year-old self, and I think my twenty-one-year-old self auditioning for *The Vagina Monologues* would do the same. I'm glad to see the consistency, and I'm even more glad to keep my momentum going. When you believe as strongly as I have in certain things like animal rights or feminism, whatever shift you create in the dominant worldview is incredibly rewarding. There is an exponentially high social reward on the investment.

Sure, I live in a bit of a bubble, and still I'm sometimes frustrated and disappointed. But I can tell the world is a different place for my son than it was when I was growing up. And I look forward to how my work, Carol's work, and the work of so many others whom we reach will continue to reshape the dominant worldview. I look forward to what's next.

STRAWBERRY-SORREL BREAD PUDDING

You might be wondering what Carol Adams had for dinner the evening she visited Vedge. While I don't remember everything that she ordered, I do remembering "crushing her with desserts," as the saying goes in our industry. One of my favorite desserts that we sent her way was the Straw-berry-Sorrel Bread Pudding. This dish is special because I conceived it for a dinner at the James Beard House in New York City back in 2010. The former residence of James Beard himself, this hallowed ground has played host to culinary icons from around the world, and Rich and I were thrilled to be the first chefs to prepare a vegan meal there for the foundation. The Strawberry- Sorrel Bread Pudding celebrates the early summer season, highlighting the classic combination of strawberries and rhubarb. I love the savory notes of sorrel and saffron here as well; they add gorgeous color to the final presentation and capture the spirit of the vegetable-focused cuisine we serve at Vedge. Serving this dish to Carol Adams, a dish I served at the James Beard House, is a wonderful honor for me on many levels.

Cake

INGREDIENTS:

3 c. all-purpose flour

1 ½ tsp. baking powder

½ tsp. baking soda

½ tsp. salt

12 oz. coconut milk

½ c. soymilk

2 c. sugar

¾ c. vegan margarine

½ stick vegan shortening

zest of ½ lemon

DIRECTIONS:

1) Preheat oven to 375 degrees F.

2) In a medium mixing bowl, sift together flour, baking powder, baking soda, and salt.

3) Blend together the remaining ingredients.

4) Add contents from blender to the mixing bowl, whisk until just mixed.

5) Transfer to parchment-lined baking pan and bake for 25 minutes.

6) Rotate the pan, then bake for 10 additional minutes or until a toothpick inserted in the center of the cake comes out clean.

7) Allow to cool for at least 1 hour before slicing. Store airtight in the refrigerator for up to 5 days.

Sorrel Sauce

INGREDIENTS:

1 ½ bunches of sorrel, leaves only

3 stalks of basil, leaves only

½ tsp. vanilla extract

¼ tsp. salt

3 tbsp. vegan margarine

¼ c. agave

¾ c. soymilk

3 tsp. egg replacer powder

DIRECTIONS:

1) In a food processor, pulse sorrel, basil, vanilla, and salt until herbs are coarsely chopped.

2) Add the margarine, then pulse again.

3) Meanwhile, in a small bowl, whisk together the agave, soymilk, and egg replacer.
4) Transfer the contents of the bowl into the food processor and pulse again to combine evenly.
5) Store airtight in the refrigerator for up to 3 days.

Rhubarb Nectar

INGREDIENTS:

4 c. chopped fresh rhubarb	1 c. sugar
	1 c. water

DIRECTIONS:

1) In a medium saucepan, simmer all ingredients on medium heat until the rhubarb is soft, about 5 minutes.
2) Transfer to blender and carefully blend for 30 seconds or until smooth.
3) Allow to cool, then store airtight in refrigerator for up to 1 week.

Saffron Ice Cream

INGREDIENTS:

2 c. sugar	18 oz. coconut milk
2 c. water	18 oz. soy milk
1 tsp. saffron	¾ tsp salt

DIRECTIONS:

1) In a medium saucepan, bring water and sugar to a slow boil for about 5 minutes to make simple syrup.

2) Remove from heat, then add saffron and let cool for about 20 minutes.

3) Transfer to blender and combine with remaining ingredients.

4) Churn in ice cream machine according to manufacturer's instructions.

5) Freeze. Store airtight in the freezer for up to 1 week.

To Assemble the Final Dessert

1) Preheat oven to 350 degrees F.

2) Cut 2 c. fresh strawberries to a ½-inch dice.

3) Cut the cake into ½-inch squares.

4) In a medium mixing bowl, toss about 3 c. of cake squares with the diced strawberries and about 1 c. of the sorrel sauce.

5) Transfer to a baking pan and heat in oven for about 10 minutes.

6) Scoop ½ c. portions of the warmed bread pudding onto serving dishes.

7) Streak the dishes with rhubarb sauce and a scoop of the saffron ice cream.

8) Serve immediately and enjoy!

Afterword

BY KARA DAVIS

*A*publisher walks into a bookstore and strikes up a conversation with the young woman behind the counter. It sounds like the beginning of a joke, but it was the spark for the book you're reading now.

Contributor Kate Larson works at Inquiring Minds Bookstore in New Paltz, located in New York state's Hudson Valley. When Lantern publisher Martin Rowe was visiting the store, Kate gave him a copy of her zine, "no better than apples," which he brought back to Lantern's offices in Brooklyn. In the zine was a personal piece about meeting feminist icon Kate Millett, best known for her 1970 book *Sexual Politics*.

The piece depicts two women, young and old, the incredible respect and intimidation that exists when meeting someone of such significance to one's herstory, having to defend one's lifestyle to that person, and the chasms that can exist between women identified as feminists. Though there is awkwardness and difference, it shows the strong connection between generations, the sense that someone else out there *understands*.

When my colleagues at Lantern and I envisioned the creation

of this book, we laughingly called it *The Sexual Politics of Meat: The Next Generation*. We liked what that sci-fi title implied: innovating feminist animal rights theory taken into the future by 20+ years of ideas applied by younger thinkers. Carol, in her original foreword, asked that her book be a stepping stone for more thought about race, class, gender, species, and the relationships between oppressions and power structures. With this anthology we've tried to take her up on that offer.

The Lantern office is filled with people who respect Carol and her book: Martin Rowe went to work for Continuum Publishing specifically because they had published *The Sexual Politics of Meat*; editor-at-large Evander Lomke edited the book at Continuum, as well as some of Carol's later works. I was an early reader, and credit Carol (and a handful of other truth-tellers) for my ability to see clearly and to think critically.

I read *The Sexual Politics of Meat* while watching the first Gulf War on a tiny black-and-white borrowed television; during the time my Tucson chapter of Queer Nation carried mock Hooters billboards in demonstration (our brand was "Peckers" and featured a gay man in his tighty whities serving soy dogs); and around the time of my first arrest at the Greyhound Racing Park entrance after learning about "retired" dogs sent to the university's cancer center to test the effect of inhaling fumes from Air Force jets. I was struggling to come out, and to understand the violence around me.

For me, the power of Carol's book is in naming. As with other important feminist texts, she lays out what she sees, examines it, and names it. We are all too used to language that hides meaning instead of illuminating it. For that reason, *The Sexual Politics of Meat* falls into a canon of beautiful words, beautiful ideas, no matter that what she describes is painful. Thank the goddesses she said those words! Like many women, when I read the book I craved hearing from people who told the truth in whatever way they could. If you can't understand what's happening when you live in an insane world, you feel insane. Understanding makes problems actionable, and the search for beauty reasonable.

Defiant Daughters assumes some familiarity with Carol's book and her theories. We are not attempting to summarize or explain her ideas, but rather to build on them and talk about what they look like in individual women's lives. The contributors to this anthology range in age from seventeen to their early forties, and their experiences with and exposure to Carol's work is varied. As can be expected, some writers learned of Carol's work in their college years, as I did. Some were introduced to it by men—brothers, lovers, and friends— and that is no surprise. As Carol points out, a world free of sexist and speciesist violence (and, of course, class and race violence) is a benefit for men as well as women and animals.

When contacting potential contributors I expected to have my mind blown by the uncharted subjects women would write about. Experiences I imagined could be relevant were a vegan in prison; a trans woman taking hormones or a woman modifying her body through surgery and binding; a circus performer; a nanny, home-care giver, farm hand, house cleaner, or another imported laborer of color; someone who is pro-porn and pro-bondage; or a teenaged girl living in a shelter with a total lack of privacy. Writers engaging with this topic could not be afraid of messiness or conflict. There are many contemporary approaches to discussing the fragmentation of women's bodies and lives, and those easily lead to discussion of the sexualization and consumption of animals. We wanted pieces for this book that came to the conversation from a personal perspective and could shed new light.

Our anthology contains discussion of concepts that didn't exist when *The Sexual Politics of Meat* was published. Nobody was yet talking about "happy meat," and, as far as I know "crip" had not yet been taken back as a political term. And, in 1990, nobody categorized themselves or others as "cisgendered." But, as Carol notes in the forewords to both her tenth and twentieth anniversary editions of her book, there is so much that has not yet changed, and the examples of the sexual politics of meat have been reused and reinforced; neither the world Carol envisioned nor some of the analyses I'd hoped to see have yet come about. We are far too busy fighting the same fights.

What many pieces in the book offer are fascinating details about how the sexual politics of meat are experienced by particular women. We learn about how specific cultural and religious backgrounds or bodily abilities can change how someone "reads" an event, and how drug use and rape can obliterate a sense of self, making it hard to extend compassion to others (that is, hard up until the point that the need becomes more obvious than ever). We learn about how parenting affects our views of the treatment of animals, and how being a businessperson in contact with a variety of customers reminds us of the ways progress has been made, and where it hasn't. We hear about the sexual politics of meat in terms of art making, performance art, and art curation, as well as teaching and advocacy. In *The Sexual Politics of Meat* Carol writes about women denying themselves food but does not explicitly talk about eating disorders; some of our contributors do talk about them, reflecting the understanding that they are a common experience of women and girls. Some of these writers (and, ahem, editors) see a connection between going vegan and coming out of the closet.

We're thrilled to share these intimate pieces with you, and

pleased to have Carol participating in the project as well. One sign of the times is that some authors feel no need to explain *why* the topic they are discussing is relevant to *The Sexual Politics of Meat*'s premises. We are meant to have progressed enough in our thinking to understand. But there is still a great deal of work yet to be done, and future generations to inspire. Zines, skill shares, and grassroots efforts like Occupy have been a wonderful source of cheap, DIY idea sharing: what forms will future thinkers use and teach us with? In what ways will our feminist and anti-speciesist conversations gain more nuance, more specificity? How can you challenge Kate Millettt or Carol Adams or the "defiant daughters" who wrote for this book?

We at Lantern are hoping that this project doesn't end with the publication of *Defiant Daughters*. Like the hundreds of people that have sent Carol ads, photos, and bumper stickers over the years, there's plenty of room for continued discussion of the relevance of the sexual politics of meat, in new and innovative applications. Please follow our conversation at facebook.com/DefiantDaughters, and show us the NEXT next generation!

About the Contributors

CAROL J. ADAMS is the author of *The Sexual Politics of Meat: A Feminist-Vegetarian Critical Theory*. It's been called "groundbreaking" and "pioneering" (interesting how our description of books draws from our invasive relationship to the land). Many say it is an underground classic, which may mean that lots of people know and love it, but it goes unnoticed by the dominant media. As an undergraduate in the early 1970s, Adams worked to bring women's studies courses to the University of Rochester and was involved in protesting the Vietnam War. She attended Yale Divinity School, where she did her fieldwork at the Women's Liberation Center and an abortion clinic. She's worked on poverty, racism, and sexism issues at an advocacy agency in New York, and started a hotline for battered women. She challenged the government to identify and prosecute domestic violence and racism in housing practices. She lives with her partner and Holly and Inky, two rescued dogs, just outside of Dallas. Besides continuing her feminist-vegan writing, she's writing a book about the experience of reading Jane Austen and being a caregiver, as well as coediting an anthology with Lori Gruen on ecofeminism and intersectional theory and activism.

SARAH E. BROWN is a writer based in Philadelphia. She has written for *Curve Magazine, Flavorpill, Vegansaurus,* and other publications, and authors the blog *Queer Vegan Food* (queerveganfood. com). She is a graduate of Vassar College.

KARA DAVIS is the managing director of Lantern Books. She is a street activist who got her start with the Sanctuary Movement as a teen in Arizona, and worked for many years with Act Up and Fed Up Queers in New York City. She recently attempted some food activism in the "locavore" crazy Hudson Valley by accepting food stamps for pickled vegetables, fresh tofu, seitan, and nut cheese at the farmer's market and running a sliding scale vegan C.S.A. She is a proud volunteer at the Catskill Animal Sanctuary, and lives in a crumbling old house with her girlfriend and too many rescued cats.

MELINDA FOX is a seasoned grassroots activist who cofounded the longest running animal activist student group at the University of Florida. She honed her professional fund-raising career in Washington, D.C. where she's held executive-level fund-raising and strategy positions in renowned advocacy organizations working on animal protection, women's health, and girls' empowerment. Prior to relocating back to the Northwest, she worked in business development for the world's fastest growing social action platform—Change.org. Today, she's a principal fund-raising strategist with Virtuosa Partners and a social entrepreneur developing an exciting mobile application called TILT, where in one touch, she connects movie ticket buyers with women in film. She credits *The Sexual Politics of Meat* as a defining framework of her activism and ethical life, considers Carol a feminist mentor, and shares the tattoo "Eat rice have faith in women" with anthology cocontributor Carolyn Mullin. Follow @ FoxMelinda on Twitter to stay in touch.

ROCHELLE M. GREEN is an assistant professor of philosophy and the University of Arkansas–Little Rock. Her primary areas of research include feminist philosophy, social and political philosophy, and 20th-century continental philosophy.

JENNIFER GRUBBS is an anarchist anthropologist at American University. Her research examines the intersections of privilege and exploitation with species relations, the neoliberal corporatization of academia, and the political repression of animal and earth liberationists. Despite that jargon-filled research summary, she remains committed to creating theory that also matters to those outside of university walls. Jennifer uses the blogosphere to politicize her personal experiences with pregnancy and motherhood at thoughtsofapregnantvegan.wordpress.com. Feel free to contact her at jennygrubbs@gmail.com.

RUBY HAMAD is a Lebanese-Australian writer and sometime filmmaker. She has written for most of the major Australian news publications including *The Sydney Morning Herald*, *The Age*, and *The Australian Broadcasting Corporation* (ABC). She is an associate editor with the progressive feminist website The Scavenger (thescavenger.net/). You can read her thoughts and reach her on Twitter (@rubyhamad) and on her blog, at rubyhamad.wordpress.com.

KATE JACOBY is the coproprietor of Vedge Restaurant in Philadelphia. A self-taught pastry chef and certified sommelier, she oversees front of house operations for the city's premier vegetable restaurant. With her husband, chef Richard Landau, Kate has helped shape the vegan culinary scene in Philadelphia for more than twelve years. At their former restaurant, Horizons, they authored two cookbooks: *Horizons: Gourmet Meatless Cuisine* and *Horizons: New Vegan Cuisine*, and they have a new Vedge cookbook due out in the spring of 2013. Kate is also the mother of Rio Jacoby-Landau, and together with her family she enjoys traveling to find new inspiration to continue evolving the restaurant and work on new projects.

KATE LARSON has been writing and self-publishing her personal zine, *No Better Than Apples*, since 2005. She plays music, eats abnormally large breakfasts, pickles jalapenos, writes strange letters to celebrities, and arm wrestles semi-professionally in New York's Hudson Valley. She never ever wants to stop making things. You can find her at teamkate.com.

WENDY LEE is the publishing director of Lantern Books. In addition to spending more than ten years in publishing, she has worked as an English teacher in China, led creative writing workshops, and served as a mentor with the nonprofit Girls Write Now. She is also the author of *Happy Family* (Grove Press), which was named one of the top ten debut novels of 2008 by Booklist. She lives in Astoria, Queens. Please visit her website at wendyleebooks.com.

ASHLEY MAIER serves as training and technical assistance coordinator for the California Coalition Against Sexual Assault's PreventConnect project, a national online project dedicated to the primary prevention of sexual assault and domestic violence. Although Ashley hails from Illinois, her work against gendered violence has taken her to Missouri, Oregon, and California. She holds a master's of social work degree from Washington University in St. Louis and a bachelor's degree in psychology and French from the University of Illinois. She cofounded and codirects Connect the Dots, a project that promotes and builds capacity to address the connections between human, animal, and environmental well-being. For more information visit connectthedotsmovement.com. Ashley resides with her partner and two rescue pugs in North Hollywood, California.

COLLEEN MARTELL earned her doctorate in English with concentrations in American literature and feminist theory from Lehigh University in Bethlehem, Pennsylvania. Her research focuses on embodied acts of resistance to oppression in feminist writing and activism, most recently from a transnational perspective. She currently teaches in Lehigh University's women's, gender, and sexuality studies program. She can be reached at cmme@lehigh.edu.

CAROLYN MERINO MULLIN is the founder and executive director of the National Museum of Animals & Society (NMAS). She has over thirteen years' experience in the nonprofit sector—at both the local and national level—with special emphasis in children's education, animal protection, and museums. Carolyn earned her bachelor's in religious studies, with a focus on religion and nature, from the University of Florida and has a master's in nonprofit management from Regis University in Denver, Colorado. See what Carolyn and NMAS are up to at museumofanimals.org.

KATY OTTO is a musician and social justice worker. She graduated with a bachelor's in journalism from the University of

Maryland–College Park, and later received a master's in nonprofit management from Trinity University in Washington, D.C. She has over fourteen years of experience in violence prevention, women's issues, youth development, and the arts. Two and a half years ago she moved to Philadelphia from Washington, D.C., and began focusing on her communications consulting work. She runs her own independent record label Exotic Fever Records (exoticfever.com) and has toured internationally with her current band, Trophy Wife (trophy wifetheband.blogspot.com). She cofounded the national Visions in Feminism conference (vifcollective.com). She has done sexual assault prevention and survivor solidarity work and workshops.

MARGARET (MEG) PERRET is a radical, queer, multiracial, vegan, anticapitalist, feminist nerd living in Berkeley, California, where she is studying gender and women's studies at UC–Berkeley. Meg's academic meanderings most often involve the messy entanglements of the biological and the cultural; however, her thoughts are always embedded in critical race theory, gender and sexuality studies, and a commitment to radical decentering of dominant discourses. Meg loves irony, deriving math equations, complaining about capitalism, defending second-wave feminism, imagining conversations with Donna Haraway, sparring with NPR programming, whispering to trees, finding new independent bookstores, and vegan cooking with her girlfriend. Meg hopes to be a university professor and bring some fresh vegan-feminism into the academy.

DALLAS RISING is an abolitionist animal liberationist, which may sound snooty, but really isn't; it's just that those fancy words most accurately describe how she approaches the many issues surrounding animal exploitation. Thanks to the Internet and digital recording equipment, you can hear her talk about all sorts of topics on the podcast she cohosts, Midwest Vegan Radio. She lives in Minneapolis with her husband, two dogs, and two cats, all of whom she is crazy about.

MARLA ROSE is a writer, activist, and community builder based in the Chicago area. She writes at her blog, Vegan Feminist Agitator, and is an award-nominated freelance feature writer. Her first novel, *The Adventures of Vivian Sharpe, Vegan Superhero*, was published in May 2012. She is also cofounder of the Chicago Vegan Family Network and Chicago VeganMania. In 2009, she and her husband were recognized as Activists of the Year by Mercy for Animals.

VIDUSHI SHARMA is a senior in high school in New Jersey. Growing up in a vegetarian household in a community bordering the Hackensack River and wetlands, she has been enthusiastic about vegetarianism and environmental preservation all her life. Vidushi is a happy student of the classics and calculus alike and enjoys creating art, playing tennis, and reading. She can often be found travelling between Ridgewood, Secaucus, and New York City on the train—usually with her sketchbook as a companion. She has worked for two summers as an intern for Lantern Books.

JASMIN SINGER is the cofounder and executive director of Our Hen House (ourhenhouse.org), a multimedia hub of opportunities to change the world for animals, named by *VegNews Magazine* as the 2011 Indie Media Powerhouse. Jasmin is also the cohost, along with her partner Mariann Sullivan, of the popular Our Hen House podcast. She is a contributing writer for *VegNews Magazine* (vegnews.com) and was also named by *VegNews* as one of twenty stand-out stars of the animal rights movement. Jasmin has been featured in various media outlets, and most recently appeared as a guest on *The Dr. Oz Show*. She is the former campaigns manager for Farm Sanctuary, and has presented widely on the subjects of animal rights and veganism. Jasmin and Mariann live in New York City with their pit bull, Rose.

DARLENE SMOOT holds a bachelors degree in philosopy and religious studies from California State University–Fullerton. She is current working on her master's in philosophy at San Diego State University. Her areas of academic interest are in continental philosophy, including feminism, critical animal studies, race, and class.

KIM SOCHA holds a Ph.D. in literature and criticism and works as a community college English instructor. She has published scholarship in the areas of critical pedagogy, surrealism, critical animal studies, atheism, and Latino/a literature. As her avocations, Kim has assisted survivors of domestic violence and sexual assault in their recoveries and now works with recently paroled sex offenders through a transformative justice program. As a social justice volunteer, she primarily works with educational programs in juvenile detention facilities and jails. Kim is also an animal liberation advocate and sits on the boards of the Institute for Critical Animal Studies and the Animal Rights Coalition. Her book *Women, Destruction, and the Avant-Garde: A Paradigm for Animal Liberation* was published in 2011 (Rodopi), and she is coediting and contributing to *Confronting Animal Exploitation: Grassroots Essays on Liberation and Veganism* (McFarland & Company Publishing, 2013), a collection of essays by Twin Cities activists. She welcomes contact at kimberlyannsocha@ gmail.com.

SUNAURA TAYLOR is an artist, writer, and activist living in Oakland, California. Her artworks have been exhibited at venues across the country, including the CUE Art Foundation, the Smithsonian Institution, and the Berkeley Art Museum. She is the recipient of a Sacatar Foundation Fellowship, winner of VSA's Driving Force award, an Eisner Award, two Wynn Newhouse Awards, a Joan Mitchell Foundation MFA Grant, and an Animals and Culture Grant. Her work has appeared in *Monthly Review, Alternet, Yes Magazine,* and *Qui Parle.* She worked with philosopher Judith Butler on Astra Taylor's film *Examined Life* (Zeitgeist, 2008). She is also an artist contributor to Rebecca Solnit's book *Infinite City: A San Francisco Atlas.* Taylor has given more than a dozen talks at universities and conferences across the country and has appeared on NPR's *All Things Considered,* Georgia Public Television's *State of the Arts,* and numerous other radio programs. She's currently working on a book on animal rights and disability, forthcoming from the Feminist Press (2013). She received an MFA from the University of California–Berkeley in the field of art practice in May, 2008. Taylor is a cofounder of the disability arts collective Yelling Clinic. sunaurataylor.org

LAURA WRIGHT is associate professor of postcolonial literature in the English department at Western Carolina University. She is the author of *Writing "Out of All the Camps": J. M. Coetzee's Narratives of Displacement* (New York: Routledge, 2006 and 2009), *"Wilderness into Civilized Shapes": Reading the Postcolonial Environment* (Athens: University of Georgia Press, 2010), and *Visual Difference: Postcolonial Studies and Intercultural Cinema* (New York: Peter Lang, 2011). She is currently at work on a book entitled *The Vegan Body Project: The Cultural Construction and Performance of Vegan Identity* (veganbodyproject.blogspot.com), for which Carol Adams is writing the introduction.

LAGUSTA YEARWOOD is a restless, rabble-rousing chef-turned-chocolatier who's in love with deep flavor, ethical sourcing, farmers, the food poor people around the world have always eaten, lactic acid fermentation, and noodles. She lives in a little 1960s sunny ranch house in the tiny farm-focused town of New Paltz, New York, with her sweetheart Jacob and three cats: Sula, Noodle (told ya), and Cleo. After years of cooking in dinky rented kitchens, she and Jacob renovated a former laundromat in downtown New Paltz to become a tiny little chocolate shop, Lagusta's Luscious (lagustasluscious.com), which opened in June 2011.

About the Publisher

LANTERN BOOKS was founded in 1999 on the principle of living with a greater depth and commitment to the preservation of the natural world. In addition to publishing books on animal advocacy, vegetarianism, religion, and environmentalism, Lantern is dedicated to printing books in the U.S. on recycled paper and saving resources in day-to-day operations. Lantern is honored to be a recipient of the highest standard in environmentally responsible publishing from the Green Press Initiative.

LANTERNBOOKS.COM

green
press
INITIATIVE

Lantern Books has elected to print this title on Enviro,
a 100% post-consumer recycled paper, processed chlorine-free.
As a result, we have saved the following resources:

16 trees, 746 lbs of solid waste, 6743 gallons of water
11 million BTUs, and 1469 lbs of greenhouse gases

As part of Lantern Books' commitment to the environment we have
joined the Green Press Initiative, a non-profit organization supporting publishers in using fiber that is not sourced from ancient or
endangered forests. We hope that you, the reader, will support Lantern and GPI in our endeavor to preserve the ancient forests and
the natural systems on which all life depends. One way is to buy
books that cost a little more but make a positive commitment to the
environment not only in their words, but in the paper that they are
printed on. For more information, visit greenpressinitiative.org.